To Cecil Currey
with admiration, affection,
and warm wishes
Forrest McDonald
Jan 21, 1975

The Phaeton Ride

Phaeton/n./ (L., fr. Gk. *Phaeton*): a son of Helios permitted for a day to drive the chariot of the sun and struck down with a thunderbolt by Zeus to keep the world from being set on fire.

Other books by Forrest McDonald

The Phaeton Ride

THE CRISIS OF AMERICAN SUCCESS

Forrest McDonald

DOUBLEDAY & COMPANY, INC.
GARDEN CITY, NEW YORK
1974

Library of Congress Cataloging in Publication Data

McDonald, Forrest.
      The Phaeton ride; the failure of American success.

      1.   United States—Economic conditions.   2.   United States—Economic
policy.   I.   Title.
HC106.M18   330.9'73
ISBN: 0-385-04305-8
Library of Congress Catalog Card Number 73-21159

Contents

Prologue

The Summer of Seventy-three

IN THE SPRING, as the daffodils gave way to the lilacs, the most awesome economic boom in history had entered its twenty-second month and was still gaining momentum. Wealth was multiplying and spreading at a rate that defied comprehension. The Council of Economic Advisors revised its estimate of the year's gross national product again, this time to $1 trillion 200 billion—a figure so large as to be meaningless, save perhaps to orthodontists and basketball players.

On the corporate level, the fruits of American capitalism had never been so plentiful. General Motors moved ahead of Sweden, Mexico, and Brazil, producing goods with a dollar value greater than the gross national product of those entire nations; its revenues were larger than those of the government of Great Britain, and it employed more workers. Ford was outproducing oil-rich Venezuela and

Iran, and Jersey Standard, Texaco, Gulf, U. S. Steel, General Electric, Du Pont, Westinghouse, and a host of other corporate giants each produced more than the GNPs of most nations in the world.

On the personal level, Americans were engulfed in affluence. Having become, a decade earlier, the first people in history to be spending less than half their income on food, clothing, and shelter, they were now past masters at lavishing their money on nonessentials. Even the poorest were likely to have hot and cold running water, central heating, refrigerators and television sets, and automobiles; and consumption at the middle and upper ranges of the population was wondrous to behold. Assembly-line workers were paying $50,000 for homes in the suburbs, and the motive power of the lawn mowers and pleasure boats they owned was greater than the motive power of every machine in China. The sons and daughters of the middle classes, finding it chic to affect poverty, were supporting a multi-million-dollar industry that produced prefaded and preaged clothes. In the aggregate, Americans were spending enough on jewelry and cosmetics to buy the entire oil output of Saudi Arabia and Libya. They were spending enough on recreation to buy the gross national product of Australia and New Zealand combined. Tens of millions of them drove more than a thousand miles from home on their vacations, burning 5 billion gallons of gasoline and enjoying the scenic beauty of their unspoiled continent from the vantage point of 50-mile traffic jams and nature parks in which as many as 20,000 trailer-campers could be crammed at a time. Another 11 million spent much of the summer in second homes in the country. Still another

4 million went to Europe, about half of them adolescents in search of action. (More teen-agers, however, returned to nature by going backpacking in the Appalachians or the Rockies, having first laid out several millions for waterproof equipment, freeze-dried pork chop dinners, transistor radios, and other gear that Daniel Boone would have regarded as barebones essentials.) Most of the adults who ventured to Europe were pursuing what was left of the *haute* culture; it was they, by and large, who were the main supporters of the "culture explosion" that had brought the number of American art museums to more than 3000, some of them housing original paintings, and the number of symphony orchestras to no less than 1450, several of which were said to be able both to carry a tune and to keep the beat.

Nor was the affluence uniquely American. Staggering as the economic growth rate in America was, it was exceeded by the growth of Japan and Western Europe. American tourists in Hawaii found the islands overrun with scores of thousands of affluent Japanese, as if Pearl Harbor had succeeded after all; and those in Spain and Italy found that German was once again nearly as useful a second language there as Spanish or Italian. German and Japanese industrialists began building factories in America, and found that American labor (average wage $4.05 per hour) was in some places cheaper, when fringe benefits were taken into account, than German or Japanese labor.

Verily, the millennium seemed to be at hand.

SOME PEOPLE thought it was too good to last, or even to be true. Many a Cassandra among professional economists maintained that the boom had been too long and too vigorous, that if it were not cooled soon it would set the stage for a devastating recession in 1974. The New York Stock Exchange reflected such uneasiness, if not downright pessimism. General Motors, coming off a record-breaking $30-billion year in 1972, with $2.1 billion in profits, smashed all records during the first six months of 1973, and yet its stock fell by nearly a third, from 84 to around 60; corporation after corporation reported record earnings for the first quarter of the year and again in the second and again the third, and yet the Dow Jones index of industrial stocks slipped from 1052 on January 11 to 851 on August 22. Wall Street pundits attributed this curious phenomenon—business going up and stocks going down—to a variety of causes, the most common being Watergate, inflation, and loss of confidence in the dollar abroad.

The skepticism did not extend throughout the corporate business community, which was installing capital goods—the machinery and equipment for producing in ever greater quantities on the morrow—at the rate of $2 billion a week, all summer long. Nor was the sovereign consumer influenced by the betting of the smart money in New York. Suspecting (what any garage mechanic could have told him) that the 1973 automobiles were the worst Detroit had ever produced, he nonetheless bought more than 11 million of them, if only on the theory that they would probably be even worse and would certainly be more expensive next year.

To be sure, two flukish events in early summer were enough to give even consumers pause, though they soon

4

recovered their aplomb. The first was an unprecedented heat wave that sent temperatures into the 90s in the Middle West and on the eastern seaboard from Washington to Boston. The consumers were prepared for just such a contingency, having spent several billions in air-conditioning virtually every enclosed space, but the power companies were not. Power failures, blackouts, and brownouts were experienced throughout the area; electric and gas compaines curtailed their institutional advertising, designed to warn the American public against the peril of government ownership and regulation, and directed their advertising instead toward urging people not to buy so much of their product. Few people turned their air conditioners off, but the heat wave passed and that was that. With admirable foresight, the power companies prepared themselves to prevent a recurrence of the episode: their strategy was, next time simply ration power. (Coincidentally, as the heat wave ended some utilities got something they had been seeking for a long time. Late in June the Federal Power Commission's control of natural gas prices was removed in certain parts of the country. In one day the price of natural gas in those areas increased 75 percent.)

The second disconcerting episode of the early summer was intimately related to the first, though few people made the connection. When all those vacationers set out in their shiny new automobiles, they were fully prepared to cope with overheated engines and defective carburetion, but they were a bit taken aback to learn that nearly half of the filling stations in the country were shut down or rationing gasoline. That was so unexpected, indeed so unreal, that most motorists refused to believe it even as they sat stranded on the turnpikes. Knowing there could not possibly be a gasoline shortage in America, the consumer perceived instantly that the gigantic oil corporations were manipulating the supply to increase prices and run the little operators out of business. The attorneys general of thirteen states, echoing the popular widom, brought or threatened to bring antitrust suits against the major oil producers. The gasoline shortage, however, unlike the heat wave, did not go away.

Of those Americans who were concerned about the state of the economy, the most powerful was Arthur F. Burns, beloved chairman of the Federal Reserve Board. Mr. Burns was an adherent of a quaint school of economic theory, not unrelated to the Austrian school pioneered by Ludwig von Mises, whose principal American guru was Milton Friedman, professor at the University of Chicago and sometime advisor to President Nixon. The Austrians held that the cause of most evils in this world is an excess of money; their remedy was to demonetize everything but gold, of which there was enough in the world to transact American business for perhaps a week. Mr. Burns was not so extreme; he merely held that the primary malaise plaguing the American economy was inflation and that inflation results not from too much money but from too cheap money. Accordingly, he spent his summer striking down the demon of cheap money by raising interest rates.

During that summer—between May and September—the banks responded to Mr. Burns's prodding by raising the prime rate from less than 6 percent to an even 10. The prime rate is the interest your friendly neighborhood

banker charges for loans to customers named Ford, Rockefeller, and Mellon. Real-life borrowers were paying 12
and 13 percent.

Bankers loved Mr. Burns and praised him for his
patriotism and wisdom, and it was only coincidental that
they customarily make a lot of money when interest rates
are rising. He was less beloved among operators of savings
and loan associations, for most of their money was out on
long-term mortgages at lower interest, and to attract de-
positors in a rising market they had to pay higher interest than they were collecting. By late August, hundreds
of savings and loan associations had their backs to the
wall, prospective victims of the same kind of money
crunch that had long since devasted the consumer finance
companies. Nor were corporate businessmen entirely de-
lighted by the monetary situation. With the market for
stocks down, corporations which could not generate capital
funds out of earnings were forced either to curtail expansion or to borrow money at higher rates than they were
earning.

In the fifty-nine-year history of the Federal Reserve
System, the manipulation of interest rates had never curtailed inflation and had rarely curbed a boom. It did
neither in the summer of seventy-three, for indescribably
grand and powerful forces were at work.

Two summers earlier, in the vast reaches of the Pacific,
massive ocean currents had shifted their courses in various
ways. One school of meteorologists attributed to those
shifts the cold winter of 1972–73 (which by an inexorable
chain of events brought on the summer's gasoline short-

7

age) and also attributed to them the heat wave of June and another in September, which precipitated the power shortage.

In the Southern Hemisphere the cool Humboldt Current was displaced, off the Peruvian coast, by the much warmer Nino Current. As a consequence, the 1971 spawn of anchovies was reduced to one seventh of normal, and the 1972 catch was reduced by three fifths. The spawn was again abnormally low that year, and by the spring of 1973 the world's supply of fish meal—widely used as a protein food supplement for cattle—had been reduced by a million tons. One principal buyer of Peruvian anchovies was Japan, whose people consumed them directly as a protein, their other principal protein source being soybeans, which they bought mainly from the United States. To compensate for the reduced anchovy supply, the Japanese placed unusually large orders for American soybeans. By mid-June Japanese demand seemed about to leave Americans short of soybeans, which they used to feed beef cattle and for a variety of other purposes.

Because grain crops are to a considerable extent interchangeable, the shortage of soybeans put pressure on existing supplies of other grains, especially wheat and corn. For many years American wheat and corn had been overabundant, so much so that their prices would long since have collapsed, but for a system of crop restrictions (whereby some 50 million acres of grain land were kept out of production) and price support programs (whereby the government bought up the surpluses and used them to feed the poor, support school lunch programs, and rescue nations threatened by famine). But just now there was no surplus, for a year earlier the Soviet Union, facing crop failures, had bought a quarter of the entire American wheat crop of about 1.6 billion bushels. It was subsequently revealed, to the embarrassment of many, that the Russians had bought the wheat at the subsidized price of $1.65 a bushel while American consumers were paying the market price of $2.75—but revelation of that fact did not return the wheat or alleviate the pressure in the summer of seventy-three.

American cattle raisers, already squeezed between rising costs and a price freeze on beef, saw the prospect of profitable sales disappear with the enormous increase in demand for grains. The Nixon administration steadfastly refused to lift the price freeze, but to protect the cattle raisers President Nixon declared an embargo on the export of soybeans. A week later export controls were extended to forty-one more agricultural products, mainly animal feeds. The order was made retroactive to June 13, and even on orders placed before that date exporters were allowed to ship only half the amount called for in any given contract. Not until September were pre-June 13 orders allowed to be met in full.

Foreign buyers became convinced by these restrictions that, in case of future shortages, Americans would fill their orders on the basis of first ordered, first served. Accordingly, speculators the world over began to bid for American crops to be marketed months or even a year later. By July 20 more than a billion bushels of future American wheat production had been sold for export, along with 1.4 billion bushels of corn, 600 million bushels of soybeans, and comparable volumes of other commodities.

By summer's end wheat was selling for $5 a bushel, and prices of other grains had risen in the same proportions.

In these circumstances large numbers of cattle raisers simply refused to sell their cattle, waiting instead until September 12, when the freeze was scheduled to be removed. Every day the cattle remained off the market cut still deeper into the grain supply, pushing prices further up and ensuring still higher beef prices when the freeze was lifted. Meanwhile, in the absence of adequate beef, American housewives turned to other meats; the sudden excess demand for chicken sent its unregulated retail price (which had risen earlier in the year from 39 cents to 69 cents a pound) soaring to $1.29, and the price of pork and fish rose apace. In the month of August—the month when farm prices normally begin to fall—the price of farm products rose 20 percent.

This spectacular chain of events was by no means due merely to the activities of governments and speculators. Argentina, Chile, Greece, Egypt, Russia, India, and China—among others—were suffering grain shortages and looking to the United States to buy wheat. In Pakistan floods brought the threat of starvation to as many as 1.5 million people, and the customary call for help from the United States government fell on deaf ears, for the government's cupboard was bare, or nearly so. In drought-plagued west central Africa as many as 12 million people had to be written off as hopeless, doomed either to death by starvation or what was possibly worse, to permanent mental and physical impairment because of malnutrition.

Thus with the world clamoring for their products, the American farmers climbed aboard the prosperity bandwagon, joining the workers and businessmen and professional people who had been passengers for some time. And the boom roared on.

THAT WAS THE SUMMER of seventy-three. Remember it well, and cherish the memory, for things will never be that good again.

Chapter I

The Corporate Revolution

AMERICANS, having known nothing but abundance, have always found it easy to cherish the notion that material well-being can be extended to all mankind. Gradually that illusion spread over the globe, for in the last two centuries the dynamics of Western culture have made possible a staggering increase in "wealth," which is to say in the production and distribution of goods and services that we regard as economically desirable. Only recently has it become manifest that we are approaching, if we have not already reached, the outer limits of what the Western way can do. The limits are there, partly because our cultural system is incredibly wasteful and the planet's resources are finite, and partly because the institutionalized aspects of the system have begun to work at cross-purposes. What this means is that we are not going to reach the millennium—not now, not soon, not ever. Man has been hungry, cold, and at the mercy of the elements throughout most of his history, and so will most of humanity remain.

To understand how we came so close and why we failed, we must take a cultural, institutional, and historical perspective. It is not necessary to have a background in economics or economic theory, and probably not even helpful. All schools of economic thought current in the Western world are based upon the false premise that something called "economic reality" dictates the forms that our social and political institutions can take. In Marxist jargon the "forces of production," meaning the way people make their bread, determine the "relations of production," meaning their governmental, religious, and social practices. In American lingo a man has to make a living first; only afterward does he think about voting or praying, and the way he makes his living shapes the way he votes and often the way he prays as well.

History and thoughtful observation show that it is just the other way around: what we regard as economic reality is determined by our attitudes, our habits and institutions, our taboos and prejudices, our religions, our culture, and above all our history. Western man, for instance, universally reckons cattle, oil, and gold as being among the most real of economic realities. Yet Indians starve to death surrounded by cattle, because their culture does not define cattle as food; to the Zulus, oil is mere mud in the ground, for they have neither the institutions nor the technology to treat is as anything else; and gold is a rock like any other rock, less useful than others for purposes of hunting, more useful for making rings and filling teeth, and having value dependent upon which a society regards as more desirable.

The rise of the Western world began with a change in its attitudes about making money. Christendom had been taught in its Holy Scriptures that the love of money is the root of all evil. This bit of palpable nonsense is abundantly refuted elsewhere even in the Bible, but for many dreary centuries a priest-ridden Western civilization was paralyzed and impoverished, at least in part because the operation of the profit motive was discouraged, hampered, or flatly prohibited by law and by institutional inflexibility. Then, at the dawn of the modern epoch—not long before the Columbian discoveries—Western man slowly began to realize that the desire for profit could in fact be the wellspring of great good. The principle was as simple as it was profound: it is that the free interchange of goods for private profit can better serve the material needs of society than can community spirit, force, prayer, or love of mankind.

Before this radical principle could become fully operative, a long process of institutional evolution had to be undergone. The very concept of private property had to be developed and implemented; commerical and other personal property had to gain equal status with land in reckoning wealth and power; realistic bookkeeping systems had to be worked out; a flexible system of money, based upon credit rather than gold and silver, had to be devised; and so on.

The nations of the Western world made the requisite institutional changes—shedding their old ways and adopting the new—at different rates and to different extents. At first the city-states of northern Italy took the lead, but after the Protestant Reformation in the sixteenth century it was generally the Protestant countries, and especially Holland and England, that made the changes most rapidly and successfully. Conversely others, notably the Spanish-speaking nations, never fully made the transition.

During the nineteenth century the United States, having inherited the English institutional tradition and, what was nearly as important, being blessed with a continent that abounded in potential wealth, was more innovative than any other nation. To be sure, even in America the acceptance of the profit motive was not complete: some cacophonous voices continued to be heard, some archaic institutions and prejudices survived. But on the whole, the pursuit of wealth became a veritable religion in America, complete with a liturgy and a system of moral values, ethics, and taboos that governed the relations between society, property, and the individual.

Alexis de Tocqueville described the American spirit as follows: the European, he wrote,

touches at different ports in the course of a long voyage; he loses precious time in making the harbor or in waiting for a favorable wind to leave it; and he pays daily dues to be allowed to remain there. The American starts from Boston to purchase tea in China; he arrives at Canton, stays there a few days, and then returns. It is true that during a voyage of eight or ten months he has drunk brackish water and lived on salt meat; that he has been in a continual contest with the sea, with disease, and with weariness; but upon his return he can sell a pound of tea for a halfpenny less than the English merchant, and his purpose is accomplished.

Henry Adams put it a different way. Idealism and materialism were inseparable in America, he wrote, and if this were understood, the American could properly be regarded as the most idealistic man on earth. The European saw the world as a vale of misery, and resigned himself to it; the American looked at a savage wilderness and saw boundless acres of grain and magnificent cities, in a future world that he and his would make—and set out to make it. Impelled by this vision, even the humblest immigrant was caught up in the American spirit, "for every stroke of the axe and the hoe made him a capitalist, and made gentlemen of his children." Of such stuff are continents conquered.

William H. Vanderbilt put it more pungently. When a newspaper reporter asked Vanderbilt what the public would think about a particular action he proposed to take with his New York Central Railroad, Vanderbilt, nonplused as well as irritated, replied with the classic line, "The public be damned." He was not expressing contempt for the people, as has usually been believed, but merely stating the generally held proposition that private business decisions were none of the public's affair. Had he been a more moderate man, he might have said, instead, "What a man does with his property is not properly the concern of anyone but himself. The public interest will best be served if every person will pursue his own interests, and not concern himself with the interests of others." That would have conveyed his meaning more accurately— though the statement would scarcely have made Bartlett's *Familiar Quotations*.

The spirit described by Tocqueville, Adams, and Vanderbilt—the love of money—transformed the United States from a raw wilderness into the richest, freest, and most powerful nation in the history of the world; and did so in less than a century and a half. Then, in the depression of the 1930s, the Americans found it necessary to make a fundamental readjustment in their economy, for the economy had become incompatible with their deeper values. The spirit underlying the change was captured in these moving words from John Steinbeck's *Grapes of Wrath* (1939): "There is a crime here," Steinbeck wrote, describing the plight of the California Okies, "that goes beyond denunciation. There is a sorrow here that weeping cannot symbolize. There is a failure here that topples all our success. The fertile earth, the straight tree rows, the sturdy trunks, and the ripe fruit. And children dying of pellagra must die because a profit cannot be taken from an orange." No one, as far as I am aware, arose to protest that, had it not been possible to take a profit from an orange, the trees would not have been planted there in the first place.

But such a comment would have been irrelevant: the trees were there, and children were dying of pellagra, and the values of the culture dictated that the rules of the economic game be changed so that children and oranges could get together. The essence of the changes was that government entered as an active participant in the economy, its goal being to ensure that those who lost out in competition for the dollar would also be provided a decent livelihood.

That commitment was as fateful as it was noble and grand. The old commitment, to survival of the fittest in the pursuit of wealth, had propelled the economy beyond the limits of the cultural value system; in the quarter century after Steinbeck wrote, the new commitment made possible an enormous broadening of the base of American wealth and a reinvigoration of the health of the entire society into the bargain. But there were other and less wholesome changes inherent in the new commitment as well: somewhere along the line it became perverted, and the tail began to wag the dog. The original idea was that the desire for profit would continue to drive the economy and an altruistic government would see to it that everyone benefited, but at some point profit-making became a dirty word.

By the mid-1960s politicians and pundits—following the lead of the children's crusade—were criticizing business-men and labor unions alike for seeking higher profits or wages, as if that were the wickedest of sins. By the late sixties pundits and politicians, speaking in the name of the public, felt free to demand that the great business corporations rectify every manner of social evil, even if it meant sacrificing profits or tackling problems that the corporations had no part in creating. What was more peculiar yet, the great corporations were often wont to comply with such demands, crying *mea culpa, mea culpa.* Thus the Chrysler Corporation, though trembling on the brink of failure, took upon itself the burden of training and hiring thousands of unemployables, people who cannot bring themselves even to catch a bus at the same time every day; and Henry Ford II put his prestige and his company behind a billion-dollar effort to salvage the rotted and economically nonfunctional downtown area of Detroit; and the Congress of the United States, prodded by the likes of Ralph Nader, required the automotive industry—already noncompetitive in international markets, where the United States already suffered devastating imbalances of trade—to add antipollution gadgets that would make American cars more expensive and less efficient, and on top of that proposed to cope with a perilous fuel shortage by a system of graduated taxes on inefficient engines. Meanwhile, the ecologist Barry Commoner demanded, as a means of heading off the imminent exhaustion of the usable fossil fuels, that air travel of less than 200 miles be prohibited, and that people be required to use trains instead—apparently without noticing that the railroads are for practical purposes deceased, having been strangled by being legally denied the opportunity to earn profits.

All this is a foretaste of what is coming. In the end, everybody gets a million dollars, but nobody can buy anything with it, for no one can afford to make anything to sell, and no one will sell what little he has.

THE PROXIMATE BEGINNINGS of the present crisis, and of the surge of the United States toward world preeminence, are to be found in the last quarter of the nineteenth century. The institutional instrument of that surge was the corporation, a legal fiction evolved mainly under the Anglo-Saxon system of jurisprudence, whereby an artificial "company" of persons is vested with the legal status of a single natural person. The process by which it evolved shaped its ultimate form. In England the earliest corporate charters—special grants of privilege from the sovereign to groups of individuals—were given to municipalities, the first being William I's grant to the City of

London in 1066. The corporation, in that sense, was borrowed from Roman and Frankish law. In the next few centuries various states and sovereigns of northern Europe and the Low Countries experimented with using the device to promote international commerce, and in the 1550s the Tudor monarchs of England began to employ it toward the same end, chartering a number of trading companies. The Stuart kings did so on a larger scale throughout the seventeenth century, and the practice steadily spread after the Glorious Revolution of 1688.

The effect of these early charters was to stimulate economic activity by liberating and diversifying it. In the medieval world (here I simplify an enormously complex subject) every person's place and function had been fixed by law and custom. The yeoman, the cotter, and the lord were born and died with the same relationship to the same land; the barrel-cooper was licensed only to make barrels and was not allowed to branch into related fields of carpentry, and the woolen merchant was not permitted to deal in other commodities. When Mary Tudor, Queen of England, vested the Muscovy Company (in 1555) with the privilege of trading in all commodities with Russia, she was in effect creating a monopoly, but—more significantly—she was also broadening the range of permissible economic activity, and so it was with other corporate charters.

In what became the United States, circumstances altered tradition, and though most of the colonies began as corporations, there was no especial need for other English-style corporations before independence. The most important altering circumstance was the ratio of land to people:

in Europe low, in America extremely high, which is to say that in America land was relatively cheap and abundant and labor was relatively scarce and dear. It was therefore impossible to implant in America a fixed system of status, and long before 1776 British-Americans were accustomed to regarding physical and occupational mobility as *rights*, not as privileges.

In the early years of the Republic, then, corporations or variants of them were of limited utility. For commercial ventures they were pointless, since anyone could trade in anything with anyone. What was then still an incidental advantage of the corporate form, the pooling of capital, could be and regularly was obtained through another device, the joint-stock company—whereby merchants formed "companies" whose life was limited to the single voyage of a ship or to a single speculative venture in land or government securities.

In one area, however, corporations were both useful and necessary. Certain functions of utility to the public —such as the building of turnpike roads, the construction of locks and canals, the installation of city waterworks, and even the founding of banks—involved such large risks, such low prospects for profit, or such large pools of capital that they were unlikely to be undertaken unless special privileges, often including monopoly privileges, were given to the investors. Virtually all the corporate charters granted during the first half century of the nation's existence were issued for such public service enterprises.

Two other features of the early American experience with corporations want notice. One is the short-lived pop-

ularity of what has been called the "mixed corporation"—
companies in which one unit of government or another
was a shareholder and active partner in the corporation's
management. For better or worse, the mixed corporation
was thoroughly discredited in the 1830s, and faded from
the mainstream of American economic life for more than
a century. In recent years it has been resurrected, more or
less, through such corporations as Federal National Mortgage and Comsat.

The other American peculiarity was legal and is still
with us. Though the Constitution is vague on the subject,
and though the Congress has from time to time granted
corporate charters, the power to create corporations has
generally been the almost exclusive province of state governments. There are, to be sure, two constitutional limitations on this power. The first is that states are forbidden
to "impair the obligations of contracts," and since 1819,
when Chief Justice John Marshall rendered his decision
in the case of *Dartmouth College* v. *Woodward*, it has
been held that corporate charters are in fact contracts. The
second is that the Fourteenth Amendment prohibits states
from depriving persons of property without due process
of law, and since the 1880s the Supreme Court has held
that corporations are persons under the meaning of the
amendment. Otherwise, however, the states have a virtually free hand.

Accordingly, corporate law evolved slowly and erratically. At first every corporate charter required a special act
of a state legislature. In 1811 New York passed the first
general incorporation law, permitting incorporation in
most cases simply through compliance with certain regula-

tions and payment of certain fees, and by the 1830s most other states had followed suit. Limited liability charters, divorcing owners and directors from responsibility for the actions of the corporation, began to come along in the 1830s and 1840s, but corporations were still restricted, in the manner of medieval craft guilds, to performing only those functions specifically enumerated in their charters. Thus if a company chartered to dig and operate a canal, for example, should stumble onto an improved process for making canal-digging equipment, it could not legally manufacture the equipment. "Any lawful purpose" charters, permitting corporations to engage in any activity that natural persons could legally perform, did not begin to appear until after the Civil War.

In the late 1840s and the 1850s, the pace of corporate development suddenly quickened, for a single reason: the railroad became technologically feasible. The railroad, like its technological forerunner the steamboat, had the character of a public service enterprise, but unlike the steamboat it could not be developed without enormous outlays of capital. Moreover, exploitation of the technological potential of the railroad required something that was unusual in business enterprise, a more or less permanent investment. Thus the railroad found advantageous all three of the traditional purposes for which corporate charters had been granted—public utility, pooling of capital, and permanence—plus a new one then being developed, the right of eminent domain. Understandably, every railroad that was built in America was built by a corporation.

Then came the Civil War, which some historians have interpreted as an inevitable result of the advent of the railroad. Be that as it may, the Civil War was a watershed in American economic development, and thereafter the war and the railroad operated in tandem to bring about a revolution. The railroad set off a technological revolution and the war set off a financial revolution, and together they gave birth to the century of the corporation.

The railroad impelled the technological revolution in a number of interrelated ways. At first it was thought of only as a cheap and fast means for the interregional movement of agricultural staples and light manufactures, but almost from the outset it began to have profound side effects as well. One was the actual *creation* of raw materials, particularly in the form of metals and cheap fuel. To be sure, the great Middle Western soft coal deposits, the Mesabi iron range, and the Montana copper fields were there all along, but they were just so much dirt and rock until the railroad made it possible to get to them easily and move them economically to market.

A second (and, in the beginning, seemingly unrelated) effect was the creation of national markets for heavy manufactures. Potentially the American market had always been large, for the Constitution prohibited the erection of tariff barriers between states and thus made the nation the largest and most populous contiguous area of free trade in the world. But before the advent of the railroad the national market for heavy goods existed only in law, not in fact. For example, virtually every city and town had its ironmonger (often the local blacksmith), who produced iron from low-grade bog ore and made it into implements for local use. Since iron products could not be moved over appreciable distances economically, and often not at all, the local producer was protected from competitors in other places, as they were protected from him. A maker of wood-burning iron kitchen stoves in one part of the country, for instance, might make his product for half what it cost the local producer in another, and yet the transportation barrier precluded competition between them. Every producer being thus confined to a limited, monopolized market, none had any incentive to search for or adopt technological innovations associated with either improved quality or larger-scale production. The railroad dramatically changed all that: the inefficient producer in upper New England or central Tennessee suddenly found himself facing potential competition from efficient producers in Pittsburgh.

A third effect was that the railroad, as a consumer, created a huge demand for the products of improved technology—especially in the areas of iron and steel production, steam engines, and telegraphy.

As the railroad erased the transportation barrier, a veritable flood of inventive activity swept America. By the 1870s the Bessemer process of converting pig iron into steel, which had been developed independently in the 1850s by the American William Kelly and the Englishman Henry Bessemer, began to be adopted on a large scale, and that (together with the railroad itself) made it possible to exploit the rich, high-grade iron ore deposits of the Lake Superior region and the bituminous coal deposits of the Middle West. Development of the steel and coal industries made possible and created a demand for huge and efficient steam engines, which was most sensationally met with the Corliss cross-compound reciprocating steam engine. The Corliss engine, in turn, stimulated the growth of the machine tool industry, and soon the great electrical inventions began to appear. In that manner the inventive process, once started, was self-accelerating: every new invention made another both possible and necessary.

Naïvely assuming (as Americans still assume) that technological innovation would make life easier without necessitating fundamental changes of accustomed ways, the entire nation became caught up in a craze for technical development. Newspapers—fed information by the growing network of telegraph lines, printed on a mass scale by recently developed web and high-speed rotary presses, and soon to be set by the revolutionary linotype machine—carried regular features on the latest technological developments, and popular scientific and technical magazines flourished. The application of ingenuity became a full-fledged profession, and hundreds, even thousands, of Americans spent their entire time trying to invent things. The most successful of them all, Thomas Edison, described the spirit that impelled them: "I'm not a scientist," he said proudly, "I'm an inventor. Faraday [the Englishman who discovered the principle of electromagnetic induction, which made Edison's inventions possible] was a scientist. He didn't work for money. . . . Said he hadn't time to do so. But I do. I measure everything by the size of the silver dollar. If it don't come up to that standard then I know it's no good." And that standard was effective: between 1878 and 1884 Edison alone invented the multiplex telegraph, the mimeograph machine, the incandescent lamp, the multiple electrical distribution system, the transmitter that made the telephone practical, the phonograph, and the motion picture, and discovered the principles that made radio and television possible. Others, including Bell, David, Harvey, Houston, Brush, and Singer, were nearly as prolific. The United States Patent Office, which Congress had seriously considered shutting down in the 1830s on the ground that everything had been invented, issued four times as many patents in the 1860s as it had previously issued in its entire seventy years of existence, and in each of the next two decades the number of patents doubled again.

But invention was only half the game, for technology without capital is as meaningless as natural resources without technology or markets. The institutionalized ways of raising capital in America, while quite adequate for the needs of a prerailroad society, were far from adequate to finance the capital-intensive industries brought about by the new technology. New York had had a stock exchange since the 1790s, for example, and there were smaller exchanges in a dozen other American cities; and an elaborate and efficient credit mechanism for financing international trade had flourished since the War of 1812. Through such instrumentalities European capital had been steadily pumped into an America that was woefully short of liquid wealth, and by a somewhat fraudulent means the United States also managed to avoid being perpetually in hock to Europe. That is to say, huge European credit balances, accruing from both capital investment and a favorable balance in the American trade, were periodically erased in financial panics, in the wake of which Americans reneged on their commercial debts by going bankrupt and bought up European investments at a fraction of what the Europeans had paid for them. As indicated, this system worked well in the prerailroad age but was entirely inadequate thereafter.

A new system was made possible by the financial revolution triggered by the Civil War. The war created an enormous pool of potential liquid capital in the form of $2.7 billion of public debt and another $400 million in wartime greenback currency. Since the early eighteenth century, when the Bank of England had stumbled onto the technique of using public debt as the basis for money, and since 1790, when Alexander Hamilton had adapted British techniques to American circumstances, wars in the English-speaking world had had the effect of increasing the money supply on a grand scale; and the American Civil War did so on the grandest scale the United States had yet known. One result was to bring into being financial houses whose operations were of a magnitude ten to twenty times as large as those of the greatest prewar houses. The biggest and most spectacular house of all, that of Jay Cooke and Company in Philadelphia, was wiped out in the panic of 1873, but others—including Lee, Higginson of Boston, Drexel, Biddle of Philadelphia, and J. P. Morgan and Kuhn, Loeb of New York—survived and thrived. Such firms, in the 1870s and 1880s, evolved into modern investment banking houses, and it was mainly they who financed the technological revolution in America.

Investment banking was distinct from both stockbrokerage and ordinary or "commercial" banking. Stockbrokers did little, directly, in the raising of capital; their real function was to facilitate the capital-raising efforts of corporate promoters by providing a market for the trading of corporate stocks that already existed. Investment bankers did most of the capital-raising, and did so in a highly specialized way. They did not lend money to corporations or buy their stock; rather, they sold, on commission, corporate securities (mainly bonds) to other buyers. Most commonly, they were men who moved into the field after establishing European connections as merchants or in some other way. The founders of the house of Kuhn, Loeb and Company, for example, had built sizable fortunes as tobacco merchants based in Louisville, Kentucky; they retired to New York and only gradually and incidentally moved into investment banking. Others succeeded because they had connections with European financiers, as August P. Belmont had with the Rothschild family, and as Henry Villard had as agent for wealthy Germans in Frankfurt and Hamburg. J. P. Morgan was the son of J. S. Morgan, partner in a firm in London that had close and long-standing ties with most of England's great commercial and financial houses. By 1885 that connection—together with young Morgan's own ability, his early ties with an old Philadelphia banking family in what became the firm of Drexel, Morgan, and the fact that once he became established in New York he had a number of partners whose astuteness was extreme—propelled the House of Morgan into a position of leadership among American investment bankers. Morgan had two additional advantages over most of its rivals. Most of them ordinarily preferred to deal in bonds rather than stock, though usually they did handle both; and since commercial banks could not legally engage in investment banking, most had no affiliation with commercial banks. The House of Morgan dealt indiscriminately in both types of securities; and since it remained a private bank, a partnership whose members disdained to seek a charter under either national or state banking laws, Morgan was legally able to combine the commercial with the investment banking function.

The requirements of the capital market thus established in turn dictated the financial forms that corporations could evolve. Two general descriptions of permanent corporate securities became common: those representing what is variously called risk, venture, or equity capital, being the shares of "stock" held by the owners of the corporation; and bonds, representing money borrowed by the corporation against a mortgage on all the corporation's property.

Gradually, refinements of each kind of security were worked out. Generally speaking, manufacturing enterprises were less capital-intensive—that is to say, required a smaller capital investment in relation to receipts from the sale of their products—than were railroads and other utilities. On the average, gross sales of manufacturers equaled capital investment in six to twelve months, whereas the gross revenues of utilities took three to eight years to equal capital investment. Utilities, on the other hand, were far safer investments, and therefore their credit was better. Accordingly, innovations and refinements of the forms of equity capital came mainly with manufacturing corporations, and the principal innovations in the forms of debt capital came with utilities.

Equity capital, over the years, came to have two main forms, common and preferred stock. Common stock represents ownership of the corporation, proportionate to the number of shares held as a percentage of the whole number of shares outstanding; the stockholder is entitled to his proportionate share of votes in electing the directors, who in turn choose the officers, and to his share of all the corporation's net profits after operating expenses, taxes, and interest. Preferred stock, originally, carried with it a fixed dividend if it were earned, plus cumulative rights to any unpaid dividends, plus a share in profits above the fixed dividend; and it also entitled holders to voting rights equally with common-stock holders. By 1900, however, preferred-stock holders ordinarily received the fixed dividend if it were earned but nothing more, no matter how large the corporation's profits, and had no voting rights unless dividends were skipped for a stipulated period, usually a year.

Bonds are certificates of indebtedness, sold in specific denominations, normally $1000. Their holders are paid a specified rate of interest, normally twice a year, and after a specified number of years the corporation is required to repay the holder the amount of the original loan. In the early days investors were leery of corporate bonds and required that they mature in short periods (ten to twenty years), be protected by "sinking funds" or partial annual repayments of principal as well as by the mortgage, and be limited to fixed amounts—much as home mortgages are financed today. By 1900, however, bond finance had become nearly as flexible as common and preferred stock: maturity dates were set for as long as forty and fifty years, sinking funds were abandoned, and open-end mortgages came into general use—permitting indefinite future expansion of debt, so long as depreciation reserves were established and the bonds outstanding amounted to no more than 50 to 75 percent of the value of the mortgaged property. (In recent years "debentures"—roughly the same thing as bonds except that they are not secured by mortgages—have tended to replace bonds in utility financing. In 1972 American Telephone & Telegraph and its subsidiaries had outstanding $21,228,326,000 in long-term debt, mostly debentures, at interest rates ranging from 2.75 percent to 8.75 percent and maturing at various times between 1973 and 2002.)

Holders of bonds and debentures have first call on a corporation's revenues after taxes and such operating costs as raw materials and wages have been met, but if their interest is promptly paid, the stockholders, as the owners of the corporation rather than its creditors, are entitled to all the remaining earnings. Moreover, bondholders have no voice in management unless interest or principal payments are in default. Finally, bonds, like stock, are freely negotiable: the corporation's obligation is to the current holder of the security, no matter how often it changes hands.

Such a financial structure gave the corporation a life apart from its owners and creditors, and when a few more features were added through legislative enactments and court decisions, the emergence of the corporation as a "person" and as an economic instrument of unprecedented flexibility was complete. Limited liability laws were common by 1880. The Supreme Court, in the case of *Santa Clara County* v. *Southern Pacific Railroad*, ruled in 1886 that a corporation was a person under the "due process of law" clause of the Fourteenth Amendment. "Any lawful purpose" charters became common about the same time, and three years later New Jersey passed the first law allowing corporations to own the stock of other corporations. In 1895 the Supreme Court ruled, in *U.S. v. E. C. Knight Company*, that manufacturing was not commerce under the meaning of the Constitution, and was thus exempt from the regulatory power of Congress,* and that monopoly was not a "conspiracy in restraint of trade" under the Sherman Antitrust Act, since a monopoly is one and it takes two or more to conspire. Two further stones remained to be laid in the corporate edifice—"no par" common stock laws, the first of which was passed by New York in 1912, and the national corporate bankruptcy act of 1934—but otherwise the evolution of the corporate form was substantially complete by 1900.

When it reached its mature form the corporation was the most potent economic institution yet perfected, and that includes the nation-state with its power to tax. Independently of the individuals who owned or managed it, the corporation could manufacture any goods or perform any services that individuals could legally manufacture or perform; it could hold, buy, or sell property, even in the form of other corporations; it could borrow or lend money, or sue and be sued. Its capital stock could be expanded or contracted, almost without limit, but no matter how much the stock was changed or exchanged the corporation itself was unaffected. When it failed to meet its obligations

---

* Since the 1930s the Court has redefined "interstate commerce" to extend to virtually all economic endeavor, and thus the regulatory power of the federal government comprehends the entire economy.

or violated the law, it could be hauled into court, judged, and punished, without its owners and managers being held personally responsible. Such an instrumentality could perform economic feats that were previously impossible, create untold wealth, and distribute wealth more widely than wealth had ever been distributed before. Without the corporation or a social invention like it the fantastic technological revolution and economic expansion of the late nineteenth century, and America's unprecedented productivity in the twentieth, would have been impossible.

The most obvious of the miracles the corporation wrought were in the heavy industries: production of iron ore doubled every decade, from 3.8 million tons in 1870 to 57 million tons in 1910; steel production increased from 1.2 million long tons in 1880 to 23.5 million in 1910; the miles of railroad track in operation increased from 52,922 in 1870 to nearly 200,000 in 1900, and ton-miles of freight hauled increased from about 8 billion in 1870 to about 80 billion in 1890; production of soft coal increased from 20 million tons in 1870 to 478 million tons in 1913. At the time of the Civil War the total power of prime movers in the United States was only about 13 million horsepower, and of that nearly two thirds was animal power. By 1880 steam power exceeded animal power, by 1900 steam engines constituted nearly two thirds of a total of 65 million horsepower, and steam power doubled again before the outbreak of World War I. Overall, the gross national product increased from $9.1 billion in 1881 to $40.3 billion in 1914, and corporations accounted for the greatest portion of the increase by far.

Less obvious were the broader social benefits. Cliché has

it that the industrial achievements were wrought at the expense of workers and the urban masses, but the cliché does not square with the record. During the years 1880 to 1910, for example, the number of jobs in nonfarm occupations increased from 8.8 million to 25.7 million, which enabled the United States to absorb immigrants, most of them adult males immediately thrust into the job market, at a rate of 617,000 a year for the three and a half decades ending with the outbreak of World War I, and 800,000 a year between 1900 and the war, while absorbing an equal number of migrants from American farms to cities—and to provide jobs for them all. And despite this tremendous expansion of the work force, in the appropriate years for which we have reliable figures (1890–1914) wages of the individual urban worker rose 50 percent, and they would double again during the war years.

Moreover, though the awesome expansion of the new industrial cities caught municipal governments totally unprepared, American business enterprise overcame a great deal of the ensuing discomfort. Thus in urban housing, for example, despite what one reads about the overcrowding of immigrants in tenements, the construction industry performed well enough so that the percentage of nonfarm Americans living in owner-occupied houses increased from 37 percent in 1890 to 42 percent in 1920; two thirds of the houses during those years were mortgage-free, which suggests that, but for the governmental impediment of federal banking restrictions, virtually everyone could have owned his own home. In addition, the advent of the streetcar, electric and gas lighting, and centralized urban water supply (all but the last being furnished almost exclusively

35

by private corporations, and even water being so supplied in large measure) made urban transportation cheap and fast, made indoor living cleaner and more comfortable than ever before, and made life in large cities less perilous to health than it had been at any time in human history.

BUT THERE WAS A CATCH to it, or rather a pair of catches. One was that it provided Americans with a vastly improved means of indulging their least lovable habit, the wanton destruction and waste of nature's bounty. Not that the corporations themselves were especially wasteful or destructive. It was not corporations who annihilated the buffalo and the passenger pigeon, denuded the forests of Wisconsin and upper Michigan, stripped the ground cover off the Great Plains and made much of that area unfit for habitation by man or beast, and ravaged the once fertile soil of the South out of greed for profits in cotton and tobacco; all that had been done by the common man without the aid of any form of organization. But to place an instrument so powerful as the corporation in the hands of a people so rapacious boded ill for the land: it was like arming locusts with jet engines and power saws.

The other catch was institutional. The emergence of the corporation as an institutional innovation of unparalleled viability thoroughly disrupted what might be called the ecological balance of American culture. Earlier, the various segments of American society—its communities, churches, schools, politics, and government as well as its economic enterprise—had been free to interact without the interference of any genuinely great concentrations of power. Indeed, one of the cardinal tenets of the American credo was that great concentrations of power were inherently evil, and doubly so if the power were based upon governmental privilege, as was certainly true of the corporations. And yet if the American people, for those reasons, found it difficult to live with the corporation, they also found it impossible, because of their commitment to the pursuit of wealth, to live without this social invention that could generate wealth so readily.

What they did was entirely in keeping with the American character: accept the irreversibility of history (what's done is done), avoid fundamental problems, ignore contradictions, and go on from there. What that implied was that noncorporate portions of the society would have to adapt to the corporation by imitating it, by seeking to devise institutional innovations of a comparable quality and scale. In time, the whole society would become what amounted to a complex of corporations.

As they did that, however, the Americans had to make another institutional adjustment: they had to reconcile their total commitment to the pursuit of money with a seemingly incompatible tradition of hostility to business.

Chapter II

The Populists and the Predators

IT WAS NO SURPRISE to nineteenth-century Americans that
the legal impediments to corporate development were removed only gradually and erratically. Rather, the surprise
was that they were removed at all, for the United States
had, before the corporate revolution, a long history of
deliberate efforts to prevent economic development, a history that involved some of the nation's most respected
statesmen and hordes of its scurviest politicians. The resistance derived from cultural inertia, from the peculiarities of the American political system, and from a strange
system of social values that made it possible for Americans simultaneously to worship the Almighty Dollar and
to hold to a revered tradition of suspicion and hostility
toward commercial enterprise.

American business came under vigorous attack, both
rhetorical and real, during the so-called Populist period of

the 1890s, and the rhetorical (though not the real) attack continued throughout the so-called Progressive period, 1901–17. Nor did it end there: in 1936 Franklin Roosevelt announced that businessmen hated him and said, "I welcome their hate"; in 1948 Harry Truman campaigned against Wall Street instead of his opponents, and was reelected; and we can expect more of the same in the next congressional elections.

Such attacks, then and now, reflect both the tone and the substance—and often the very language—of a movement that began nearly two centuries ago. Nothing is quite so embarrassing, as someone said, as the pedigree of ideas. The wellspring of the radical antibusiness mentality in America was the reactionary English Tory Henry St. John, Viscount Bolingbroke, and his equally reactionary circle of friends. Bolingbroke is best remembered for his Jacobite plots, through which he hoped to undo the Glorious Revolution, dethrone the Hanoverians, and return the discredited Stuart dynasty to the Crown of England. He is more worthy of memory, however, as the center of a group which included Alexander Pope, John Gay, and Jonathan Swift, and which coined the modern philosophy of anticommercialism.

During the first half of the eighteenth century, and especially during the ministry of Sir Robert Walpole (1721–42), English society became thoroughly commercialized, in what has been called the Financial Revolution. The essence of the transformation was the monetization of public debt through the instrumentality of the Bank of England, and the subsequent monetization of society. Suddenly land ceased to be the sole basis of wealth and power, personal relationships ceased to be fixed, and a love of gambling, stockjobbing, and speculation swept the land. No economic development in England's history, not even the enclosure movement or the industrial revolution, was half so disruptive of traditional English society and values.

Bolingbroke and his circle saw nothing but decay and evil in eighteenth-century English life, and saw money as the poisonous wellspring of it all. More precisely, he attributed the evil to the monetization and commercialization of all human relationships. Earlier, he maintained, relations between Englishmen had been based upon ownership of the land, honest labor on the soil, craftsmanship in the cities, and free trade on a small scale between individual traders. Moreover, since all men were secure in their sense of place, they could also be secure in their individual identities and sense of values. Accordingly, honor, manly virtue, and public spirit governed their conduct, and ambition and greed were regarded as the cardinal vices.

Upon the advent of the Financial Revolution, however, people were caught up in a frenzy for money, and with this frenzy came a passion for bigness—whether in the form of gigantic privileged monopolies, oversized government, or standing armies—which depersonalized relationships, injured the small landowner, trader, and laborer, and alienated all of them from any sense of place, of value, of meaning. As a result, virtue succumbed to a love of luxury and vice, public spirit gave way to secrecy and deception, to materialism, extravagance, venality, and corruption. Honest toil was no longer rewarded; the honest laborer was robbed by the impersonal forces of money, and only the dishonest, those who lived by cunning and artifice, could thrive. In short, money and influence became the measure of all things; he who had them was everything, and he who had them not was nothing.

Bolingbroke wanted to turn back the clock to a romanticized past, but his philosophy and language could readily be adapted to radical ends. Doubtless what has just been said sounds familiar. In 1972 Abbie Hoffman and Rennie Davis talked like that, and so did George C. Wallace and Lester Maddox. As to the Democratic candidate for the presidency, George McGovern boasted of his rural origins, where "you have a sense of belonging to a particular place and knowing your part in it"; he denounced the moneyed classes who live "by slipping through the loopholes at the expense of the rest of us"; and he cried "Come home, America . . . from secrecy and deception in high places . . . from the entrenchment of special privilege . . . from the waste of idle hands to the joy of useful labor."

BOLINGBROKE'S IDEAS were spread and popularized in most parts of colonial America, but they took deepest roots in the South and especially in the Virginia of Thomas Jefferson. Now, the Virginians of Jefferson's generation and school were a fascinating lot of men. We celebrate them, justly, for their erudition and learning and their stirring words and deeds in behalf of American independence and human liberty. On close scrutiny, however, they do not stand up so well. They were avid in the pursuit of wealth, their principal avenues toward that end being the operation of tobacco plantations and speculation in western lands.

Their business techniques were based upon force, upon command and obedience rather than law and the exercise of wits, and indeed were scarcely distinguishable from theft and murder. Perhaps theft will be considered too strong; but what is a better word to describe taking the entire fruit of the labor of others, which is what the Virginians did to their slaves? Doubtless murder will be considered too strong a word; but how else does one describe killing people to obtain their lands, which is what the Virginians did to the interior Indians?*

Such a style—essentially that of a polite and cultivated version of feudal robber barons—served the Virginians well in Virginia and the West, but it proved entirely inadequate in the commercialized world that was aborning in the eighteenth century. The Virginians were notoriously inept in business dealings: their accounts were slipshod if they kept them at all, they lived lavishly and beyond their means, they produced far more tobacco than the European commercial mechanism could economically absorb. Consequently, they fell regularly and progressively deeper into debt; and when they were pressed for payment their characteristic resort was to fraud or force.

But they were also learned and cultivated men with pretensions to high civilization, and so they needed a more genteel rationalization for what they were about. This is where Bolingbroke came in. He sang the praises

* It is common in some quarters to go much further and charge that all American economic development was based largely upon exploiting the blacks and killing the Indians, but those ways of life were common only to the South and West and actually retarded the nation's economic growth.

of an English gentry in a precommercial world; they affected the manner of an idealized gentry, and pretended to stand above the sordidness of commercialism. He denounced the creation of privileged trading monopolies; they laid blame for their economic failure on the monopoly of English tobacco merchants established by the Navigation Acts. When their economic plight became grave on the eve of the Revolution, they simultaneously tried to extricate themselves through fraud and used Bolingbroke's language to protest everything emanating from London.

Independence gave the tobacco planters a fresh start, for it enabled them to write off approximately £2 million sterling in debts to British merchants. Soon, however, they slipped right back under; and this time, having no English monopoly to blame, they screamed that the market had been rigged against them by Robert Morris, Philadelphia merchant prince, erstwhile Financier of the Revolution, and precursor of Alexander Hamilton.

That turn of events set the stage for a legendary confrontation, in which the antibusiness prejudices of Bolingbroke-cum-Virginia gentry became enshrined into holy tablet in America. In 1790–91 Hamilton proposed his grand system whereby the nation would be inextricably tied together with sinews of commerce and finance, much in the way that Walpole had done in England. Hamilton won the backing of powerful interests the nation over by making it profitable to support the new national government, but the genius of his system ran much deeper than just that: he made the entire currency and credit mechanism of the nation dependent upon the strength and stability of the government. Upon the adoption of his

43

program, it would be inconvenient if not impossible for anyone to make a profit at anything except through the commercial and financial machinery he was creating, for that machinery was the foundation of the entire money supply. The implications were not lost on the proud Virginians: Hamilton was proposing an institutionalized stacking of the rules of the game, in favor of the very kind of free commercial intercourse in which they were unable to participate successfully. Accordingly, they gathered under the leadership of Jefferson and James Madison to destroy Hamilton's program before it could come into being.

The Jeffersonians lost in 1790–91, but they kept up the attack and a decade later they gained control of the national government. During Jefferson's presidency and then Madison's, they systematically destroyed as much as they could of the Hamiltonian system, and insinuated their agrarian prejudices into the national credo. In the simplest terms, agrarian republicanism held that the farm and farmers were good, that the city and merchants and other capitalists were bad. As if penning articles of faith for the movement that impelled thousands to take up life on rural communes in the 1970s, Jefferson piously declared that "those who labor in the earth are the chosen people of God if ever He had a chosen people, in whose breasts He has made His peculiar deposit for substantial and genuine virtue." And again, "the mobs of great cities add just so much to the support of pure government, as sores do to the strength of the human body."

Two more elements completed the anticommercial trinity. The Jeffersonians held that gold alone was money, and that debt, public or private, was inherently bad. The Hamiltonian Federalists, on the other hand, recognized that a monetized public debt could be a positive good by providing the basis for private credit, and thereby serve as the means by which a raw, rural America could be transformed into a prosperous commercial, industrial, and urban nation. Jefferson himself, and the more alert of his followers, opposed debt and credit and their various instrumentalities for precisely that reason, and the rest of the agrarians viewed the entire subject of paper transactions—government bonds, corporate stocks, bank notes, account books—as mysterious, crooked, and designed to cheat the honest worker.

The third element accounted for the great popular appeal of the agrarian creed. The vast majority of Americans were nonslaveholding farmers, and though virtually all were commercial farmers, hungry for wealth—the sturdy, self-sufficient subsistence farmer existed mainly in myth, and never as a matter of choice—few expected that they would get rich solely from wielding the ax and the plow. But the Virginia republicans offered an alternate route to wealth, namely land speculation. Acquiring large tracts of unoccupied land and selling it at a huge profit to hordes of newcomers: that was the Virginians' dream in the eighteenth century, and it became the common farmers' dream in the nineteenth. (In the twentieth, the game went urban; the heirs to this aspect of the Jefferson tradition bear such names as Babbitt, Zeckendorf, and Levitt. They pay homage to the agrarian ideal by removing the masses from crowded cities and selling them "Big

Big Quarter-acre Lots"—90 feet by 120 feet—in the green-ery of suburbia.)

Before going on, it is important to understand clearly what was at stake in the contention between Hamiltonians and Jeffersonians. If the pursuit of wealth be conceived of as a social game (or games) with rules, it is seen that the Hamiltonians were best equipped for playing under one set of rules, the Jeffersonians under quite another. The Hamiltonian rules, which were primarily (but not exclusively) suited to the North, favored commerce, fi-nance, and living by the exercise of one's wits; the Jeffer-sonian rules, primarily suited to the South, favored land, slavery, and living by the exercise of force—or more prop-erly by exercising the capacity to command. Each group tended to be contemptuous of the other, but what is more important, neither group could compete successfully un-der the rules of the other.

Hamilton sought to impose what might loosely be called northern commercial rules on the whole nation, and for a time he succeeded. The Jeffersonians sought to impose southern agrarian rules on the nation, and for a time they succeeded. After the War of 1812, Jefferson's principles and party had totally triumphed, but a modified version of Hamilton's financial system, including a Second Bank of the United States, was established as a matter of ex-pediency. Henceforth, the two sets of rules were compat-ible: one could play by either. Moreover, under Nich-olas Biddle's skillful direction, the Bank exerted a firm but gentle restraint on all activity, providing both stability and prosperity and ensuring that any talented and lucky player had a reasonable chance to win. Thus commercialism and anticommercialism could exist side by side and even complement one another, for both were consistent with harnessing individual greed for the task at hand, namely the conquest of the continent.

BUT THEN CAME THE JACKSONIANS, who destroyed this arrangement. The Jacksonians thought of themselves as heirs to the Jeffersonian tradition, and if certain allowances are made, they were right. The hard-core Jacksonians, those who formed the original basis of Andrew Jackson's support, were in fact caricatures of the Jeffersonians, exaggerations in every respect but one, and that exception made them caricatures all the more. This difference was that they were, by and large, Scotch-Irish frontiersmen—forebears of our present beloved rednecks—instead of tidewater Englishmen, which meant that they were lacking in the social graces and aristocratic pretensions that sometimes moderated the Jeffersonians' conduct. Thus, for example, they did not attack Indians only when they coveted the red men's land: they killed Indians for the sheer hellish joy of it, on the theory that the only good Indian was a dead Indian. Nor did they aspire to the life-style of the cultivated country gentleman; that was entirely beyond their ken and alien to their own style.

The Jacksonians democratized Bolingbrokism or the agrarian creed, whereas the Jeffersonians had merely republicanized it. Their lack of restraint can be seen in the two actions of the Jackson administration that were most directly the President's own doing: the forcible removal of the Cherokee Indians from their treaty-guaranteed lands in Georgia and Alabama, and the destruction of the Second Bank of the United States. Jackson declared that the total annihilation of the Indians would not be especially unfortunate, if the result were "progress"; and when the Supreme Court handed down a decision protecting the Cherokee in their rights, Jackson blatantly ignored the ruling with the famous challenge, "John Marshall has made his decision; now let him enforce it." Subsequently, Jackson as commander in chief oversaw the United States Army as it executed the death-march removal of the Indians to the Oklahoma Territory. As to the Bank, Jackson's message vetoing the recharter of the institution was a masterpiece of unrestrained, Bolingbroke-style demagoguery. The Bank, he averred, was rechartered by Congress "to make the rich richer and the potent more powerful"; and he denounced all such legislation as "grants of monopolies and exclusive privileges," amounting to a "prostitution of our government to the advancement of the few at the expense of the many."

In their enthusiasm for rigging the game to favor themselves, the Jacksonians went too far, and the consequence was the emasculation of the national authority. When Jackson took office three institutions constituted the backbone of that authority: the presidency, the Supreme Court, and the Bank. When he left office the executive branch was a shambles; so discredited was the very idea of a strong President that, for three quarters of a century, only one man who occupied the office dared even exert its powers to the constitutional limits. In the chief justiceship, in place of John Marshall sat Roger Taney, an utter scoundrel whose every decision favored state power over

that of the nation. In place of the Bank stood fiscal an-
archy.

The result was that the rules of the game—the trade
game, the money game, the land game, or whatever—
were thenceforth to be set by the several state legislatures.
That, in turn, proved the undoing of the South and West.
The legislatures of Virginia, Georgia, Arkansas, and the
others rigged the rules in favor of the agrarians, which is
to say in favor of force; in such states the young man of
mental agility and a commercial bent had no chance, except as an agent for outside commercial interests, and the
young man with no more assets than the habit of command had every chance. The North and East went the
other way, toward commercialism—and what was more
telling, so did western Europe. The South had locked itself into an inevitable losing position.

The Civil War only confirmed what had happened.
The southern reliance on force was no match for the
northern reliance upon brains, or more properly upon
brains directed toward and supported by commercial and
financial activity. Afterward, the agrarian tradition could
move only toward radicalism, toward a shrill challenge to
the very fundaments on which American society was
based; and in that direction it did move.

MEANWHILE, however, Jacksonian democracy had left
another legacy, the two-party system of ritual politics, in
which neither party represents anything concrete in the
way of ideology or governmental policies but each represents itself as the epitome of good, according to the
prejudices of the times, and represents the other as the

epitome of evil. The system totally mystifies Europeans, whose political parties represent bona fide ideological positions, but it is readily understood if one views it from the perspective of cultural anthropology and with a dash of skepticism. American political parties exist solely for the purpose of winning elections and dividing the spoils of victory. Since politicians can scarcely woo the electorate by admitting this and saying they want public office because it's a good job, they lie. More properly, since they —like insurance salesmen and psychiatrists—must believe in their own nostrums if they are to convince clients of their efficacy, politicians invent "issues," the best of which have nothing to do with anything substantive but can inspire frenzy in the electorate. Parties, in turn, cultivate "images," keeping them vague enough so as to house Senators Stennis and Humphrey comfortably under one roof and Senators Goldwater and Javits under the other. On those rare occasions when a politician refuses to play by the rules and honestly embraces an ideological position —as Goldwater did in 1964 and McGovern did in 1972— he gets clobbered.

The system worked admirably in Jackson's time and it works admirably in ours: its function is a kind of purification rite. Every two years (and especially every four) we vest all our frustrations and hostilities and hopes and fears in the party of our choice, regard our own as representing the forces of light and the other the forces of darkness, and do battle in the manner of a holy crusade. Win or lose, social tensions are eased, and we can carry on for a time with a minimum of domestic slaughter.

One flaw in this otherwise excellent scheme of things is

that it provides no suitable means by which politicians can be adequately rewarded for the valuable social service they perform. Thus by definition the politician's livelihood must be earned *sub rosa*. Like the priest or the witch doctor, he earns his keep by murmuring incantations and acting out a ritual—which includes the convention that politicians are disinterested public servants—and he has no choice but to profess a belief in his own magic. In Jackson's time Americans had committed themselves to the belief that any government which actively interfered in the operations of the economy could do so only by granting special privileges, thereby improperly tampering with the rules of the economic game; and politicians could succeed in their craft only by catering to this prejudice. The course that politicians must and did follow was therefore obvious: denounce special privilege publicly and grant it privately in exchange for a bribe.† It was this peculiar set of institutional realities that barred the rational development of the corporation during the last half of the nineteenth century, even in those states fully pledged to play the commercial game.

Perhaps I can make this point clear with a few ex-

---

† In our own enlightened times bribery is not especially common. The game goes on, however, through the employment of subtler devices, and virtually every successful politician except a few of those who are independently wealthy plays it. The means by which President Nixon acquired a string of mansions is a case in point. Another is the means by which Mr. Integrity himself, Senator McGovern, obtained a net worth of $271,000 on a senator's salary. And that is at the upper levels, where politics is relatively clean; in the House of Representatives, the state houses, and the city halls, practitioners of the political trades are less fussy about how they reward themselves for their services.

amples. As I indicated earlier, state legislatures were slow to adopt "any lawful purpose" corporate laws. Obviously they would be so, given the character of the political arts; when a corporation licensed to manufacture widgets under a general incorporation statute happened upon a profitable way to buy and sell gismos as an ancillary operation, it had to go begging to the politicians for a special act granting permission to do so. The politicians were apt to pass the special act if special favors were given them as individuals, and only then.

Thus in 1871, for instance, the legislature of Pennsylvania, under the control of Republican political boss Matthew Quay, passed a law vesting the United Gas Improvement Company of Philadelphia with the broadest charter ever given to a utility company in America, allowing it in effect to do anything that individuals could legally do. What the Widener-Elkins syndicate paid Quay and his subordinates for that charter is not a matter of record, but we can safely assume that it amounted, in the words of Terry Southern's *Magic Christian*, to a pretty penny. Had Pennsylvania enacted an "any lawful purpose" corporation law, such grand boondoggling would not have been necessary, and so such a law was not enacted. Nor was Pennsylvania atypical: in the year 1869 alone, for example, the legislature of Illinois sold seven hundred liberal corporate charters on a similar basis.

Occasionally, early corporation owners had sufficient *chutzpah* and skill—ability to play a game other than their own—so that they dared challenge the predatory politicians in their own arena. The legendary Commodore Cornelius Vanderbilt was one such. Politicians in Tammany Hall and Albany once conspired to revoke the charter of the New York and Harlem Railroad, without which Vanderbilt's New York Central system was worthless, for it was the system's only access to the city; and in secret anticipation of this action they borrowed every nickel they could and sold New York Central short, expecting the stock of the parent company to collapse. The Commodore got wind of the scheme and bought up every share in his company. When the New York and Harlem charter was revoked the price of Central stock did not drop, for he owned it all. He allowed the politicians to cover their short sales by providing them stock in exchange for exorbitant prices and a new charter. In the process, as he cackled afterward, he "broke the hull durned legislature."

Few businessmen were resourceful enough to fight against the irrationality of the system, however, and to most the barriers erected by politicians were nuisances to be overcome by whatever seemed the most expedient means. John D. Rockefeller, an organizational genius if ever one lived, found it far easier to impose order upon his ruthless and wily competitors in the oil business than to stay within the shifting law devised by predatory politicians. He was scarcely able to come up with a workable plan—say a pool or a trust—before politicians had enflamed the traditional popular distrust of monopoly, passed a new law making his arrangements illegal, and offered to wink at violations of the law in exchange for a private price. Not until the 1890s, when the legislators of Delaware and New Jersey implemented a scheme for attracting all large corporations to flock to their states for protection and plucking—namely the first laws permitting corporations to own the stock of other corporations—did Rockefeller find a legal means of bringing order out of chaos in the oil industry. In 1899 he formed the Standard Oil Company of New Jersey, a "holding company" which dominated the industry by acquiring controlling interests in a host of subsidiaries.

Two more examples of the irrationality of the laws— and of the process by which the corporation as an institution came into being—may be mentioned. Rarely has an inventor and entrepreneur had so much to offer mankind as Thomas Edison did with his system of central station electric light and power, and rarely has any met so many obstacles in marketing his benefaction. Edison's electrical inventions brought into existence two new industries, one to make and sell electrical equipment and the other to generate and distribute electric energy. To spread the risk and raise the necessary capital for his enterprises, Edison found it necessary to incorporate them. Several corporations were required, for part of the manufacturing was done in New York and part across the Hudson River in New Jersey, and the corporate laws of the two states were different. Moreover, the electric light company in each city had to be a separate corporation, for each had to secure in its own name a franchise from the city it served; and as Samuel Insull, then Edison's private secretary and financial factotum, recalled in an unguarded moment fifty years later, such franchises were forthcoming only after the palms of aldermen were crossed with silver. As time went by the corporate structure of Edison's enterprises became ever more unwieldy—so much so that in 1892 financiers were able, upon the formation of the General

Electric Company, to force him out of the very business he had founded, on the ground that he had mismanaged his affairs. But his successors were hardly more successful: fifteen years later, the material advantages promised by his technology had only just begun to be realized; and the principal obstacles, all the way, were political.

The final example concerns the creation of the United States Steel Company. As every schoolboy used to know, U. S. Steel was the first billion-dollar corporation, and was formed by the consolidation of most of the steel producers and fabricators in the country. It is almost as well known—or rather believed—that a large proportion of the stock of the company was "watered," which is to say that fictitious stock was issued against no tangible assets. I quote from Harold Underwood Faulkner's *American Economic History,* the most successful economic history textbook ever published: "The actual value of the tangible property of this new corporation was estimated by the Commissioner of Corporations at $682,000,000; yet it was capitalized at $1,402,846,000, of which $510,205,-000 represented preferred stock, and $508,227,000 common. Obviously, all of the common stock and an appreciable share of the preferred represented 'water.' "

In fact, what is obvious to the careful student of the political predator is that the promoters of U. S. Steel operated perfectly legitimately but were forced to appear illegitimate in order to stay within the limits of a deliberately archaic law. U. S. Steel's common stock was worth no more than $35 a share on the market, despite the efforts of the promoters to raise it, for the simple reason that investors and gamblers on the stock exchange thought it was worth no more. State law, however, required that the stock have a par value of $100, irrespective of the market price.

Visualize, then, the negotiations between the U. S. Steel promoters and the owners of, say, a wire and cable company worth $30 million. The U. S. Steel people offer $30 million, which is a fair price and one acceptable to the owners, but propose to pay in stock of the new company rather than in cash. The owners are willing but, upon checking the market, find that $30 million par value of stock is worth only $10 million, and demand $90 million in par value of stock, which is worth the $30 million they ask. The bargain is sealed, and U. S. Steel issues stock with a par value of $90 million to buy property worth only $30 million, and thus seemingly creates $60 million in "watered" stock. In actuality, of course, the steel men have been entirely honest; what was dishonest was the law, and so it would remain until no-par stock laws began to be enacted in 1912.

IN THE MEANTIME, as the corporation was emerging by fair means and foul as the most potent institution in American life, the agrarian tradition was undergoing permutations. What happened to it was that—having earlier become republicanized and then democratized—it now, representing a losing cause, became radicalized. Historians used to write about an agrarian crusade against the wicked corporations that unfolded in several phases between the 1870s and 1896. We now know that the several movements—the Greenbackers, the Grangers, the Farmers' Alliances, and the Populists—had no continuity of personnel or even of geographic source, and precious little else in common except a protest that the rules of commerce were commercial.

The radicalization of the agrarian tradition had four main consequences. One was that the continuation of the clamor kept the tradition alive, even though discredited and outside the mainstream of American development. Closely related was a second, the identification of the Democratic party with the tradition: roughly a third of the electoral votes and seats in Congress were automatically Democratic because they came from the one-party South, and any Democrat who aspired to a national majority had therefore to pay homage to the tradition of Jefferson and Jackson. Thus even after 1896, when Democrats and Populists fused in support of the agrarian William Jennings Bryan, and were so decisively defeated that farm-based radicalism never again rose as a national force, the national Democratic party was stuck with the need to identify itself with the tradition. This political necessity would return to haunt everyone in due course.

The third consequence was more subtle. The discrediting of Populism made it necessary for practical, predatory politicians to devise new ways of keeping the anticommercial tradition alive, for it was popular suspicion of business that made it possible for them to continue to play their nefarious and profitable game.

The fourth consequence was the most subtle and most portentious of all. In the various farmers' crusades, many businessmen found ways to rig the rules to their own advantage at the expense of other businessmen, and could not resist the opportunity to do so. For example, New York wholesale merchants, seeking to reduce freight rates for agricultural and industrial products shipped from the Middle West, despaired of success through ordinary means; and so in secret they not only joined but also subsidized the Granger movement in Illinois and Iowa, combining forces with retail merchants in those states to give under-the-table backing to farmer-politicians who demanded and brought about antirailroad legislation. Similarly, it was silver mining interests that underwrote the Populist crusade of the 1890s, whereby the farmer was to obtain "justice" through the free and unlimited coinage of silver at the extremely inflated rate of 16 to 1.

In sum, corporate businessmen themselves came to see advantages in the radicalization of the agrarian tradition. Viscount Bolingbroke now had some powerful advocates, indeed.

Chapter III

Brer Rabbit and the Engineers

SOME GENERATIONS ARE SKEPTICAL, others easily gulled, and there is a rhythm to the alternation. During long periods of turbulence, disorder, and change people cease to trust anybody; as someone said, there are times when paranoia is the only form of sanity. Then comes a wave of widespread prosperity, and with it comes a pell-mell rush to find a cause or a person to believe in. Every mountebank has a field day, and every form of quackery has its adherents. In those circumstances, diverse elements in the pluralistic American establishment tend to close ranks and hawk some new form of ideological wares.

Such has been the history of our own times, and so it was at the turn of the present century. In the early 1890s, after the technological, corporate, and financial revolution had been disrupting traditional ways and values for more than a generation, cynicism and violent radicalism swept

59

over the land. Then suddenly there came a calm, and then a mood of optimism, even of euphoria. Extreme radicalism was dissolved by the campaign that resulted in the election of William McKinley in 1896; a long depression was replaced by an even longer boom that began in 1897; and popular frustrations and social tensions were further relieved by the elixir of a quick and successful war that began and ended in 1898, announcing to the world that the United States had become a power among the nations. So pervasive was the new mood that even Henry Adams, a doomsayer since birth, thought for a time that he saw hope for mankind.

In this atmosphere a new strategy was evolved by the various groups that ruled America. Corporate businessmen in ever greater numbers learned that the anticommercial tradition could be turned to serve their own ends, and a new generation of politicians learned that it could be more profitable to cooperate with the corporations than to fight them. Joining in alliance, businessmen and politicians set the nation on a new course—but it was a part of their design that the sovereign people should believe themselves to be taking charge, supporting popular champions in a crusade to wrest power from the Interests and the Bosses.

So successfully was the strategy implemented that fifty years passed before a handful of historians began to tumble to what had happened. What nearly everyone long believed was that a group of reformers—Presidents like Teddy Roosevelt and Woodrow Wilson, congressmen like "Fighting Bob" La Follette and George W. Norris—instigated and led a comprehensive reform program that came to be known as the Progressive Movement. The central aim of the movement (here I quote Arthur Link, a distinguished Wilson biographer) was "to insure the survival of democracy in the United States by the enlargement of governmental power to control and offset the power of private economic groups over the nation's institutions and life."

Only in the last decade or so, thanks to the insights and perceptive scholarship of such historians as Samuel Hays, Richard Abrams, Gerd Korman, Gabriel Kolko, and Robert Wiebe, have historians finally penetrated the rhetorical smoke screen released at the time, and arrived at a fairly clear notion of what "progressivism" was all about. The nature of the present consensus among historians is implicit in one of Hays's subtitles, "The Gospel of Efficiency," and in one of Wiebe's main titles, "The Search for Order." Working hand in hand, powerful political leaders and corporate businessmen committed the United States to what became a self-accelerating drive to render society orderly, rational, efficient, and therefore more manageable. To quote myself on the subject, "Americans worshipped a machinomorphic god with technocrats as its high priests; they deified the machine and attempted to fashion themselves and their society in its image."

The diagnosis is accurate, I believe, as far as it goes; but the commitment to rationalization had its irrational elements, and in the long run those elements proved to be as powerful in shaping our modern dilemma as did the primary drive itself.

THE POLITICAL PART of the "progressive" coalition was a shifting collection of improbable partners, for politicians are of necessity promiscuous bedfellows. In reality there were two sets of coalitions, one in national and the other in local politics. In Washington the principal elements were old New York and New England aristocrats on the one hand, and hard-nosed, shrewd, tough-minded professionals who had risen to power in the Senate as representatives of great new corporations on the other. This coalition was formed largely in reaction to political corruption and radicalism; the state and local coalitions, which came to power mainly in the Middle West, largely reflected a reaction against corrupt politicians and unchecked corporations.

What all these groups shared in common was a desire to restore order. Few of them realized, at first, that in restoring order they would only hasten the rate of change, would set off a revolution which, quintessentially American, was a revolution by intensification and institutionalization of previously existing traits.

Potentially at the service of both groups of new politicians, national and local, were a host of specialists, experts in newly formed or newly reformed professions: engineers, bureaucrats, scientists, sociologists, efficiency experts, economists, conservationists, political scientists, reform lawyers. Such professions were, by their very nature, committed to the imposition of order on their own terms. Their prescription was forthright: to a man, the social scientists and would-be social engineers maintained that order could best be established through the creation of powerful regulatory commissions staffed by impartial experts, namely themselves; and by and large the new breed of politicians agreed with them.

At this point the interests and aims of the new politicians intersected those of the leaders of the great new corporations. A number of forces had been driving big business in that direction for some time. Four sets of such forces, related and yet distinct, now began to coalesce.

The first was the development of the concept of the natural monopoly, an idea borrowed from Germany, where the technological revolution was unfolding just when it was in the United States. The idea was this: whatever the merits of competition in other lines of business, public utilities could be operated sensibly only as monopolies because of their high capital requirements in relation to sales. In the railroad and gas and electrical industries every consumer had at his disposal machinery and equipment costing many millions of dollars, but used that equipment only a small fraction of the time or in minuscule quantities; consequently, the costs of servicing capital investment (interest and depreciation) were the main costs in supplying the product. On the other hand, a single investment could serve the needs of a large number and variety of customers. Thus two railroads or two electric companies competing for the same customers in a given area could not possibly supply the service as cheaply or as well as could one. Monopoly was therefore the only reasonable way to provide the service.

The logical corollary of the natural monopoly principle was public regulation, to ensure that utilities did in fact provide their product at the rates and standards of service which monopoly status enabled them to do. And there was something else: the utilities were actually being regulated already, but by predatory politicians in their own interest, rather than in the interest of either the public or the companies. Moreover, utilities were more vulnerable than other businesses: manufacturers who encountered excessively greedy politicians could often pack up and move, but utilities were fixed to a place. Accordingly, regulation by a body of impartial experts would, to utility people, bring a vast improvement over existing arrangements.

A second force emanated from what might be called naturally oligopolistic industries. In such diverse industries as oil refining, meat packing, steel making, machine tooling, and automobile manufacturing, monopoly would have stifled technological innovation, and yet the capital requirements were sufficiently large that unrestrained competition could be crippling if not devastating, to producer and consumer alike. In the oil industry, for example, prices could swing from a nickel to a dollar a barrel and back in a matter of hours, and a million-dollar investment could be wiped out in as short a time. If we think of capital as what society has been able to accumulate, to save up, from its expenditures of energy to a given point— as opposed to spending energy merely to stay alive—then such wanton destruction of capital was unforgivable. Just so, in fact, did men like John D. Rockefeller think of it.

And yet people in the oligopolistic industries did not have an easy justification for monopoly, as those in the utility industries had, and indeed they saw the virtues of competition, within limits. What the Rockefellers of the world wanted and needed was survival of the fittest: domination of their industries by those whose organizational, production, and marketing genius entitled them to positions of domination. What they had instead was political democracy—whereby, should any player prove superior under existing rules of the game, representatives of the great mass of unskilled players and nonplayers could cut them down simply by changing the rules. Thus to natural oligopolists as well as to natural monopolists the stability of regulation by impartial arbiters was much to be desired.

The third force was that of bankers, and especially investment bankers. The banker's capacity for tolerating creativity and other forms of disorderly conduct is on a par with that of the queen bee or the general, which is to say nonexistent. During the 1890s Wall Street itself was a jungle of competition between the Jewish houses, meaning Jacob Schiff and his and allied firms, and the *goyische* houses, revolving around J. P. Morgan and his allies. By 1901 order was established in the world of high finance, Schiff and his associates taking control of the financing of most railroads and streetcar companies, Morgan and his associates assuming control of the heavy manufacturing industries. After the financiers reached the agreement that divided the world into those spheres of influence, order was quickly imposed in a wide range of enterprises. Among the firms that resulted were United States Steel, International Harvester, the meat packers' Big Six, and International Mercantile Marine.

However, if the Sherman Antitrust Act of 1890 were to be taken seriously, all such industrial combinations were outside the law. For that reason, and for a variety of others, the great bankers sought legal sanction for the order they imposed. Thus they found themselves in the same camp with politicians, engineers, monopolists, and oligopolists

65

—none of whom, in different circumstances, would have been natural allies.

The fourth force derived from the other three, and from the inner needs that produced the other three. Financiers like Schiff and Morgan and corporate leaders like Rockefeller and Armour had begun to impose a measure of external organizational order upon a variety of industries, but internally the industries remained as chaotic as if unrestrained competition had continued to prevail. The fact of the matter was that people who put industrial combinations together knew next to nothing about how to manage the combinations once they were formed. As Robert Wiebe put it, "if those who thought of the new industrial giants as diabolically perfect organisms could have peeked inside, they would have found jerry-built organization, ad hoc assumptions of responsibility, obsolete office techniques, and above all an astonishing lack of communication between its parts. . . . Presiding over such ramshackle concerns, the officers could only command and hope."

Once an industry was externally rationalized—that is, brought to monopoly or oligopoly status—the attention of its managers was necessarily directed toward internal rationalization. For a number of reasons, concern with that problem disposed corporate businessmen to look favorably on an alliance with the new politicians. For one thing, their cartelized status must be legally and politically protected, for there was no point in creating an efficient internal organization if the external organization remained insecure. For another, in attempting to rationalize their managerial, production, distribution, and personnel functions, the corporate operators necessarily turned for help to the very social scientists and engineers who were already becoming allied with the new politicians. For still another, the idea of joining the coalition appealed mightily to the egos of corporate businessmen, for as the alliance moved closer toward conscious reality, talk of reconstructing the entire social order along rational lines became increasingly common. To be an integral part of such a grand design was irresistible.

Given this formidable array of political, corporate, and intellectual power, reinforced by an optimistic popular mood, it is scarcely surprising that the rationalization movement began and went so far toward succeeding.

BUT THERE WERE BARRIERS, the principal one being that there were people who preferred the old order and were willing and able to defend it. More specifically, parts of the drive for rationalization ran counter to the interests of various groups in the economy, and the entire program ran counter to the interests of old-style politicians.

As to the economic divisions, virtually every farmer and country storekeeper opposed "big business" as a matter of course, almost as a matter of instinct. Moreover, they found willing allies and leaders in the hordes of small, independent producers who, fighting to prevent being crushed by the superior capital and organizational resources of the industrial and transportation giants, made their voices heard through trade associations and such organizations as the National Association of Manufacturers—which in those days was the representative of small-business men.

Nor were big-business men themselves a single happy family—any more than they are today, despite John Kenneth Galbraith's persistent delusion of a monolithic and all-powerful corporate "technostructure." Most tycoons become what they are by virtue of a ruthless competitive spirit, and habits of a lifetime are not easily changed. Wall Street today cannot control the Cyrus Eatons or the oil-rich Texans; and even at the height of his power J. P. Morgan found it impossible to control such mavericks as "Bet a Million" Gates and difficult to restrain such of his own subordinate executives as Henry Clay Frick. What is more disruptive, various segments of the economy habitually fight others. At the turn of the century, railroadmen and oilmen regarded one another as mortal enemies, and similar (though perhaps less intensely felt) animosities separated railroadmen from merchants, importers from manufacturers, and primary producers from processors.

The antagonisms between politicians were potentially as antithetical to rationalization as were the economic rivalries. Middle Western progressives and eastern Mugwumps shared a hostility toward the entrenched big-city bosses, but also distrusted one another. Too, the Easterners attained power by reaching an accommodation with both the machine politicians and the great corporations, whereas the Middle Westerners did so only by declaring open warfare on both. The bosses, for their part, were more seasoned, more skilled, more resourceful than either set of reformers, and jealously guarded their prerogatives. That was the key to their conduct: they cared not so much about what was done as they did about doing it in a way that left them in full possession of their prerogatives.

Conditioning anything that was done, providing an element that everyone had to take into account, was the anticommercial tradition and the deeper cultural force that underlay it, human resistance to change. Though the fiasco of the Populists and William Jennings Bryan had discredited the agrarian tradition, its continuing vitality in a moderated form was clear to those who observed the way that La Follette and other reformers gained control of Middle Western states between 1900 and 1905. They all renounced Populism, but every one campaigned against the railroads, eastern capital, and the city. As to human inertia, it is programmed into man's very genes to resist transference of control over his lot to outsiders, to aliens and alien forces, and that is precisely what was implied in the movement to rationalize American life.

JUST WHO IT WAS who contrived the technique for overcoming these several barriers to rationalization, I am at a loss to say. I am tempted to think of it as the Chicago school of businessmen and politicians, for it is with the Chicagoans that I have been able to dig deepest into private primary sources and have been privileged to have had candid interviews with knowledgeable old-timers from several camps. Too, it is easy to regard Chicago as Carl Sandburg did, simultaneously as the essence and as a caricature of America.

In any event, it is clear that the main technique of reconciliation was that of Brer Rabbit. You remember Brer Rabbit: he escaped from the clutches of Brer Fox by begging not to be thrown into the briar patch, which was in fact his preferred habitat. The variation on this theme adopted during the Progressive period was that both Brer Rabbit and Brer Fox were parties to the agreement: politicians gave businessmen what they wanted, while each pretended that punishment was being inflicted by one upon the other.

A few examples will make the technique abundantly clear. For openers, let us look at the episode in which Theodore Roosevelt won his enduring reputation as a trust buster. In the winter of 1900–1 the battle between the Jewish investment banking houses headed by Jacob Schiff and the gentile houses headed by J. P. Morgan had come to a climax. The ostensible rivals were E. H. Harriman and his Union Pacific on one side and James J. Hill and his Northern Pacific and Great Northern on the other; the ostensible prize was the Burlington Railroad, whose lines ran from Chicago to the eastern termini of the three contending western roads. The actual rivals were Schiff and Morgan, and the actual stakes were control of the financing of American railroads—financing railroads being a far more profitable business than operating them. Schiff won, and future financing was divided according to the arrangement already noted. Almost incidentally, management of the disputed western railroads was turned over to a holding company, organized for the purpose and named the Northern Securities Company.

Something over a year later Theodore Roosevelt, president for six months by virtue of an assassin's bullet, instructed Attorney General Philander Knox to institute a suit against Northern Securities Company for violation of the Sherman Antitrust Act. The target was brilliantly chosen, for the general public mistakenly assumed that the company was a pet creation of J. P. Morgan which held together a great consolidated railway system. It could in fact be dissolved with no appreciable disruption in the financial community; moreover, the government's case was so prepared that if it should win (as it did in 1904) none of the financiers involved would suffer any loss and they might (as it turned out they did) even make a great deal of money by losing the case. What the ostensible victims of the action thought about it is evident from their contributions to the presidential campaign of 1904: Harriman $50,000, Schiff $100,000, and Morgan $150,000, all given to support the reelection of Theodore Roosevelt.

The Northern Securities case is a negative example of the Brer Rabbit technique: President Roosevelt gained a reputation as a champion of the "square deal" for the "little fellow" by taking an action that did not harm and actually resulted in a profit to big business. Rather more important were actions designated as antibusiness which were in fact designed in the interest of business—or, more properly, big business. Typical was the act creating the Bureau of Corporations, passed in the 1903 session of Congress: that measure was drafted by lawyers for large corporations, but became law only after Roosevelt convinced a gullible public that it was opposed by "the Rockefeller interests."

Rather the tidiest example of the Brer Rabbit technique, however, is seen in the passage of the Meat Inspection Act of 1906. Since 1891 the big meat packers of Chicago had been lobbying, unsuccessfully, for the creation of a federal commission to inspect and grade American meat. The motive of the packers was twofold. On the one hand, American meat was noncompetitive in international markets, for its quality was deservedly suspect; on the other, the big corporate packers could readily meet high standards of quality, whereas their hundreds of small competitors could not. Federal inspection (at, of course, federal expense) would therefore improve the competitive position of the big packers both abroad and at home. Efforts to bring about such inspection, however, failed regularly for a decade and a half.

Then the big packers discovered Brer Rabbit. The socialist crusader Upton Sinclair attacked them in his muckraking novel *The Jungle,* aimed at improving working conditions in the stockyards but arousing more readers by its sickening descriptions of unsanitary packing conditions in the yards. In response, the big packers financed a campaign of self-vilification. President Roosevelt cooperated by instituting antitrust proceedings (which could not be made to stick) against the major packing firms. A great public clamor arose against Swift, Armour, Cudahy, and the others, and Congress responded by passing the Meat Inspection Act of 1906—along precisely the lines that the Big Six had been advocating since 1891.

Employment of Brer Rabbitry in state and local politics was more subtle; perhaps, since local politicians were nearer to the eyes of the voter, it had to be so. The means by which electric utility companies won the status of legalized monopolies under state regulation is a case in point. Back in 1897 the Chicago traction magnate Charles Tyson Yerkes, the thinly disguised protagonist of Theodore Dreiser's *The Titan* and *The Financier,* had heavy-handedly bribed both the Chicago city council and the

Illinois legislature to approve a measure that would have transferred power over local transportation from city councils to a state commission. In the atmosphere then prevailing, perhaps such crude measures were necessary—for, after all, Yerkes was asking politicians to enact legislation that would make it unnecessary for people in his business to bribe them ever again. In any event, as fate would have it the politicians accepted his bribes but were unable to deliver, for the forces of reform chose just that moment to become outraged over an exposure of Yerkes's under-the-table dealings.

Yerkes's successor as the leading figure in Chicago utilities was Samuel Insull, the English-born former secretary and business manager to Thomas Edison, who, by 1902, was the nation's foremost electric central station operator. On a day-to-day basis Insull fended off the local politicians by various means—including setting them up in a small lighting company of their own in the red-light district—but meanwhile instituted an elaborate plan to bring about a more suitable permanent solution. Through the National Electric Light Association Insull instigated a study, conducted by the industry itself, of the relationship between government and the industry; and through the National Civic Federation he instituted a similar study by a respected impartial citizens' group. Both studies recommended state-regulated monopoly, the latter in a three-volume report published in 1907. Then the distinguished University of Wisconsin economist and labor historian John R. Commons, who had worked with Insull as one of the National Civic Federation's chief full-time investigators, drafted a law based on that experience, which the La

73

Follette progressives of Wisconsin promptly enacted. Other states followed Wisconsin's lead. In Illinois, Insull persuaded Democratic political boss Roger Sullivan to have the state legislature study the Wisconsin example, and in due course the desired legislation was introduced. Insull persuaded several of the state's utility men to oppose it, but remained out of the limelight himself. The law was passed, without the expenditure of a nickel in bribes.

Another and more devious instance of the use of the Brer Rabbit technique concerned coal mining. John L. Lewis, then business manager of the Illinois Federation of Mine Workers, struck a private deal with the Republican and Democratic national committeemen from Illinois, both of whom happened to own coal mines. They would see to the passage of serious mine safety legislation, to be enforced by a commission dominated by union members, in exchange for which Lewis agreed that all future contracts be set to expire on April 30—which meant that strikes would be largely ineffectual. The deal was advantageous to all parties but scarcely the kind that could be openly publicized, so an elaborate charade was acted out to give the illusion that there was a bitter fight between capital and labor over the passage of the law.

By means such as these, state after state established utility regulatory commissions, insurance commissions, industrial commissions, mine safety laws, and laws governing the employment of women and children; and the national government established the Bureau of Corporations (1903), the Department of Commerce and Labor (1903), the Food and Drug Commission (1906), the federal inspection of meat (1906), the Federal Reserve System

(1913), and the Federal Trade Commission (1914), and adopted a host of similar measures. Meanwhile, the consolidation of business enterprise and the internal reorganization of big business proceeded apace. The search for order, the drive for rationalization and corporate-style institutionalization of the American economy and American society, was proceeding handsomely.

THERE ARE LIMITS to the efficacy of the Brer Rabbit technique, however, and it can be dangerous to those who employ it. The greatest danger is that a campaign of self-vilification will get out of hand, that serious enemies of the sponsoring business will somehow get access to the seats of power and make life generally uncomfortable. In the mid-sixties, for example—if the editors of *Ramparts* are to be believed—the Rockefeller interests mobilized Resources for the Future, the Conservation Foundation, RAND, and various other organizations to set in motion the environmentalist movement. Their motive was twofold, to co-opt and thereby defuse the radicalism which then seemed to imperil the entire establishment, and also to profit from an assortment of bogus "ecology" legislation that could be expected in the wake of the movement.

If such a scheme actually existed, it backfired to the great disadvantage of those who conceived it. The Sierra Club (which had once had Rockefeller support) and a variety of other environmentalist groups proved to be unmanageable, and from the point of view of the Rockefellers' Standard Oil and other major oil companies, they have caused a great deal of mischief. They got court orders blocking the construction of an Alaska pipeline, and what was less publicized but more telling, they managed to block construction of refineries in much-desired locations from Maine to California. By 1973 it had become conceivable that such groups, if not brought under control, could—given the underlying general unpopularity of the petroleum industry—actually destroy the industry as a private, profit-making enterprise.

Something pretty much like that happened with the railroads during the Progressive period. The railroads were America's biggest single industry, and they not only played the Brer Rabbit game, they may very well have invented it. One of the earliest documented uses of the technique came in 1903, when the eastern roads, long harassed by Rockefeller and other great shippers who forced them to grant costly rebates, fought back through a law that was billed as punishment of the wicked rail interests. The law was the Elkins Act, forbidding rebates as if they were a devious money-making device invented by the roads themselves, but actually drafted by attorneys for the Pennsylvania Railroad and pushed through Congress by their kept senator, Stephen B. Elkins of West Virginia.

But the railroads were especially vulnerable, for a number of reasons. Most importantly, perhaps, they and nearly everyone else figured they were indestructible. The railroads were so big, so powerful, so necessary that they could be subjected to any amount of abuse and still thrive: no one believed that geese who lay golden eggs are anything other than immortal. They were, in truth, in excellent shape as the twentieth century began, having just been thoroughly refinanced, the water squeezed out of their stock issues and their bonds being refunded at low interest rates; and serious competition from the automotive and trucking industries lay a generation and more in the future. Yet indestructibility was an illusion, and a dangerous one.

In point of fact the railroads were in a perilously exposed position in the new world that was aborning. For one thing, the demagoguery of two generations of agrarian politicians—following, it should be remembered, an earlier generation which had viewed the railroads as miracle workers, and had given them subsidies at every level of government from the Congress of the United States to the humblest Nebraska school district—had left them woefully lacking in what would soon be called public relations, and the much publicized misdeeds of such operators as Jim Fisk and Jay Gould had exacerbated their bad image. For another thing, the heads of the great new industrial corporations considered them fair prey, and were quite willing to play the Populist game to stimulate government action designed to force railroads—whose freight rates had already fallen by nearly two thirds in three decades—to lower their rates still further. For still another thing, when the great oil and coal and steel interests ganged up against the railroads, the railroadmen could count on no moderating pressure from such powerful financiers as J. P. Morgan and George F. Baker, because hegemony over railroad finance had, since 1901, resided in the Jewish investment banking community, and the gentile establishment no longer felt any major concern in the area.

Finally, there was a technical problem in the railroad business that virtually no one noticed until it was too late. Regulation, in the style of the rationalization movement, made sense only for those roads which were monopolies in the territories they served. This was in actuality the status of most roads in the trans-Mississippi West, some in the South, and a few in other parts of the country. For the other roads—for example, the half-dozen lines that competed for freight over essentially the same territory between Chicago and the eastern seaboard—it would have been reasonable either to merge them into monopolies and regulate them as such, or to allow them to continue unrestrained competition. It was entirely unreasonable to insist that they continue to be fierce competitors, as the original Interstate Commerce Act of 1887 required, and yet at the same time regulate them and set their rates as if they had no competitors. But this was precisely the policy followed in the railroad legislation passed during the Progressive era—the Hepburn Act of 1906, the Mann-Elkins Act of 1910, and, with modifications, the Esch-Cummins Act of 1920.

It has been argued that irrational regulation killed the railroads by making it impossible for them to raise the new capital necessary for maintaining and improving their lines. The argument goes a bit too far; it leaves out, for example, such factors as growing competition from alternate means of transportation and the weakening of the Jewish financial community as a result of supporting the Central Powers in 1914–17. Nonetheless, when the erratic regulation of the prewar period was followed by the clearly punitive regulation that came later, the doom of the railroads was sealed.

EXCEPT FOR THE RAILROADS, however, the golden age of rationalization was at hand, and even the railroads were in for a brief improvement. Historians used to believe that the Progressive Movement died when the United States entered World War I in 1917; understanding the genius of the movement as the drive for rationalization, we now know that 1917 was a point of takeoff, not of decline.

The war itself, or more properly the way Woodrow Wilson's administration chose to fight it, gave a tremendous impetus to rationalization—and made rationalization so popular that trickery was no longer necessary. Wartime food and fuel boards, established to mobilize the economy for war, organized production and distribution on a scale that private business had not yet attempted: the food administration, under Herbert Hoover, brought such an increase in food production that the foodstuffs available for export trebled in two years, and the fuel administration, under Harry Garfield, brought about a 20 percent increase in coal production and a 50 percent increase in oil production. The Railroad Administration, under Walker Hines of the Atchison, Topeka & Santa Fe, began a rapid program of converting the railroads into a single integrated system.

Most spectacular of all were the activities of the War Industries Board, headed by Bernard M. Baruch, who became a veritable tsar of industrial production. Baruch forced competitors to cooperate, profiteers to hold down

79

prices, stubborn producers of peacetime goods to convert for war. To save strategic materials and make production more efficient, he ordered drastic standardization, down to the minutest portions of the economy: the number of styles of pocketknives was reduced from 6000 to 144 and the number of colors of typewriter ribbons from 150 to 5, restrictions such as the elimination of steel boning in women's corsets saved enough steel to build two battleships, alteration of the design of toy carts saved 75,000 tons of tin, removal of a painted line on rubbers saved 31,000 gallons of varnish. More importantly, Baruch initiated a series of studies of segments of the economy and came up with recommendations for consolidating and rationalizing business—under private ownership and management but with government supervision and cooperation—that would bring great efficiency and enormous savings. The prospects were irresistible: the creation of a privately owned, government-encouraged "superpower" electric system in the northeastern states alone, for example, would save 30 million tons of coal and $150 million a year. In sum, the economic structure of the Central Powers was being adopted to "save the world for democracy."

The momentum for rationalization, thus stimulated during the war, continued and even increased during the postwar decade. Baruch's industrial proposals became government policy, and the continuation of Hines's policies was encouraged when the railroads were returned to private management with the Transportation Act of 1920. By 1925 Calvin Coolidge was able to cackle his celebrated aphorism, "the business of America is business," and three years later the climax of the drive for efficiency and order was reached with the elevation of the "Great Engineer," Herbert Hoover, to the presidency of the United States.

In truth, the mountaintop seemed in sight: after thirty years, the rationalization movement had resulted in a staggering increase in production and an almost equally staggering improvement in the material quality of American life. But there were some by-products of the movement, too, and these would soon loom as far more important. One was that 1929 was just a year away. Another was that business and government had become partners, as it were, and businessmen were about to learn anew that politicians were not the most reliable of allies. Still another was that the employment of the Brer Rabbit technique had kept the antibusiness tradition alive, had indeed revitalized and modernized and even urbanized it.

Of the first two legacies of the movement, businessmen were unaware. Of the third some, at least, were acutely aware, and had set out to rectify it by creating a new image of the corporation as a "good citizen." That development may have been the most dangerous of all, for it thrust the corporations into a role which they were institutionally unable to play.

Chapter IV

The Corporation as Father

BUSINESSMEN WHO THINK ABOUT SUCH THINGS are wont to date their unfavorable public image from the attacks made upon them by Franklin Roosevelt and his New Deal. If one overlooks the fact that the antibusiness tradition was already two centuries old by the time Roosevelt became President, there is some merit in such a dating system. The New Deal was, in truth, the first administration in a hundred years, since the presidency of Andrew Jackson, to indulge in wholesale demagogic attacks on the very elements in the economy that made it work; moreover, since the economy was not working notoriously well when Roosevelt took office, such attacks were hardly surprising.

The fact is, however, that businessmen brought the condemnation upon themselves in quite a different way. It was not that businessmen caused the stock market crash of 1929 and the subsequent depression; that was the doing of government. Nor had businessmen caused the panics and depressions of 1819, 1837, 1857, 1873, 1893, 1907, or 1921; in every instance government policy was the principal culprit. But not until the depression of the 1930s was the business community totally blamed for what had gone wrong. A large portion of the reason was that businessmen, speaking primarily in behalf of big corporations, had convinced the American people that business was almost exclusively responsible for the prosperity that preceded the collapse. Reasonable as that position was, businessmen had never proclaimed it so conspicuously before. After the crash had come, the popular and political logic followed easily: if business in general and the big corporations in particular had brought the boom, they must also have brought the bust.

Corporate businessmen had begun to put themselves into that vulnerable position back during the early days of the Progressive Movement. Let it be recalled that the sole reason for the existence of corporations was that they were able to earn profits for themselves by supplying the public with goods or services that were better or cheaper or otherwise unavailable. When they set out to make the world over, however, that *raison d'être* no longer seemed enough. The corporations, or many of the bigger ones anyway, also set out to be, and to convince others they were, something else as well: the very best of good citizens, the keepers of everybody's brother, the Americanizer, the Samaritan, the father figure. As sensibly, economists might have set out to establish a new theology.

THE ORIGINS OF THE MOVEMENT which was sometimes called welfare capitalism are not to be found in philanthropy. To be sure, a minuscule portion of the new-

rich industrialists, Andrew Carnegie being the most celebrated of them, were extremely skillful at making money
but felt guilty about doing so, and they devised philoso-
phies of trusteeship and engaged in expensive philan-
thropies to atone for their imagined sin. Most of the win-
ners, however, either assumed with George Baer that God
had chosen them for their roles or dismissed philosophy
entirely and, like Diamond Jim Brady, lived according to
the maxim "If you have it, flaunt it."

It was those who more or less shared Baer's point of
view who instituted welfare capitalism—not as an instrument of charity but as an instrument of worker control.
Given the engineering mentality, a scientific sort of paternalism seemed the most efficient way of managing
large numbers of workers whom management not only
did not know personally but, more commonly than not,
never even saw.

The stimuli for adopting that point of view were various. One was the spread of unionization, which threatened the interposition of an outside (and nonscientific)
voice into managerial decisions. Another was the arrival
and absorption into the work force of nearly a million
immigrants a year, and what often seemed to management
the same thing, the spread of such un-American forms of
radicalism as anarchism and socialism or communism.
More potent than either of these, at least among the larger
employers—as Gerd Korman has pointed out in his study
of Milwaukee—was preoccupation with the cost of equipment and the cost of training people to use the equipment. "A happy worker is an efficient worker" was the way
one corporate executive put it. The president of Interna-

tional Harvester Company called for "benevolent despotism over the human side of manufacturing." And even the most callous corporate manager could be appealed to if it were put in this cynical fashion, as with variations, it regularly was: "Suppose," one can hear Patrick Cudahy saying, "that you have invested hundreds of dollars training some dumb mick or wop to use a piece of machinery that cost you tens of thousands, and some dumb bohunk stumbles and falls into the machinery and breaks it. Never mind the dead worker—he can be replaced—but your investment in machinery and training is down the drain."

So inspired, the great new industrial corporations began to shower their workers with unasked blessings. In addition to cleaning up their plants and making them safer and more healthful, they instituted programs offering free medical benefits, company-financed night schools, unemployment compensation, profit sharing, voluntary employers' liability benefits, workers' savings and loan associations, retirement plans, and mutual benefit associations. Such programs were normally announced through "house organs," employee newspapers or magazines designed to improve worker morale.

By 1905, of the roughly 20 million urban workers of all categories, about 1.5 million were receiving such benefits; by 1914 the number had approximately doubled. The vast majority of the workers affected by the programs were in big manufacturing companies—International Harvester, Bucyrus-Erie, U. S. Steel, Allis-Chalmers, General Electric, Armour, Heinz, Ford, Standard Oil, and others—and in the electric and gas utility industries.

Some big industrial corporations, not content with

merely establishing such programs for their own workers, sought to have them extended by law to workers in lesser industries. Many big-business men, for example, recognizing as clearly as union organizers and radicals did that intolerable working conditions were fertile breeding grounds for both unionization and radicalism, lobbied for the passage of mine and factory safety laws and legislation regulating factory conditions and establishing industrial commissions to enforce the laws. Such laws, incidentally, also benefited big business by increasing the cost structure of smaller competitors.

During and after the war welfare capitalism was extended until it affected 5 million workers, and took on two new dimensions. One was Americanization. The trauma of war dramatized the fact that the melting pot had not worked, for millions of "hyphenated" Americans had been torn by conflicting loyalties when the United States jonied the Allies. Accordingly, businessmen—and this time not merely those in the big industrial corporations, but small manufacturers and railroaders and wholesalers and retailers as well—took it upon themselves to transform their immigrant workers into patriotic, English-speaking, "100 percent" Americans. The other new dimension was that of the company union, sometimes called the Colorado Fuel and Iron Plan, after the Rockefeller company that first instituted it on a large scale. Company unions won employee loyalty through such means as fringe benefits, occasionally higher wages, procedures for settling grievances, and employee ownership programs—through which, in some instances, as many as 90 percent of the employees became stockholders of the companies they worked for.

In the short range, welfare capitalism was a whopping success. One index alone attests to the increased tractability of the labor force: union membership declined from more than 5 million to just over 3.

THE MORE PROGRESSIVE of the great corporations were by no means willing to stop there, with welfare capitalism designed to seduce and placate their workers. To them, efficiency, power, and control were not enough: they wanted to be loved as well.

The most conspicuous suitor of public favor, and for some time the most successful as well, was the General Electric Company. For three decades prior to 1922 GE had been run by Charles Coffin, a tough Yankee of the old school who had built his company into a sprawling giant and won it a great deal of public disfavor into the bargain. When it was suggested that the company seek to win good will by publicizing Coffin, he said, "Not in my time. I won't have anything to do with it. . . . A company's job is to make goods and sell them. The less said about personalities the better."

But the truth was that General Electric was in trouble, and not just with the public. The company's gross sales expanded rapidly during the war, reached $318 million in 1920, and then plummeted to $179 million in 1921, and by 1922 GE had been forced to lay off 20,000 men— nearly a quarter of its work force. In that year the company was reorganized, it went into the business of producing household appliances, its holdings of public utility stocks were transferred to a subsidiary (Electric Bond and Share) which was then spun off as an independent corporation, and its top management was placed in the hands of Owen Young, chairman, and Gerard Swope, president.

The new executives were an unlikely pair. Young was a corporation lawyer and a firm believer in publicity who had a relationship of mutual admiration with the old muckrakers Lincoln Steffens and Ida Tarbell. Swope was a veteran in electrical manufacturing (in Western Electric Company) with a background of service at Jane Addams' Hull House and its New York counterpart, the Henry Street Settlement House, and his wife was a social worker who had been John Dewey's assistant at the University of Chicago. To the business community, their appointment was scarcely less shocking than the appointment of Ralph Nader to the chairpersonship of General Motors would be today—and they lived up to expectations.

"Mr. Inside," as Swope was christened, reorganized the company top to bottom along lines that were humanistic as well as functional, while "Mr. Outside," Young, set out to woo and win the general public. In the short run, their success was phenomenal: profits, internal efficiency, and employee morale all went soaring. For our purposes, however, the immediate results are less interesting than what they did, how they did it, and what the long-term consequences were.

Swope's skill in managing people, individually or in the aggregate, has rarely been matched. Indeed, study of his techniques would afford abundant rewards for modern executives. Inheriting an entrenched bureaucracy—wherein a goodly number of people had reached their level of incompetence, in accordance with the Peter Principle—he set out to replace it with more functional arrangements. To do that, he toured his various plants and divisions incessantly, not so much to learn how things were being done as to discover competent people. When he found such prople, he kept careful tabs on what they did, meanwhile adding them to a pool of talent that he held in his head. He drew on the pool as special problems arose. Instead of forming a committee—he hated committees— he would assign the problem to one of the subordinates he had been watching. First, however, he would give the man a trial run by assigning him to study and report on a different but somewhat similar problem which Swope had already worked out. If the report was up to Swope's own standard, the man got the job and the attendant promotion.

Such methods kept the managerial hierarchy fluid, saving it from the hardening of the arteries that plagued many large organizations. Employee morale, too, was kept high, for the stultifying need to please one's immediate superior, common to most bureaucracies, did not apply at GE: the only man it was essential to please was the top dog, Swope himself. All that was needed for such a system to work was for the president to have absolute authority, an ability to judge men, and an ability to delegate responsibility. It scarcely needs adding that few executives at any time have had those three attributes.

Swope's techniques for dealing with employees in the mass were no less imaginative: his design was to convince them that they were an essential part of something larger than themselves. Part of his method was to deluge the workers with fringe benefits, after the fashion of welfare capitalism, but always to do so in a way that involved worker participation in determining the benefits and making them effective. Another part was to bombard the workers with propaganda designed to create a sense of identity with the company, and to buttress that sense with tangible interests. Toward the latter end, in 1923 Swope created the General Electric Securities Corporation: GE owned all the stock, but GE's employees supplied the Securities Corporation's capital by being allowed to buy up to $500 in its bonds annually. No fewer than 30,000 employees bought bonds; the subsidiary then bought stock of the parent General Electric Company, becoming its largest single stockholder. This was profit sharing on a strange basis, but it was effective: General Electric workers believed they were working for themselves, not Wall Street, and their morale and efficiency both went soaring. Indeed, when Swope attempted in 1926 and 1927 to promote a company union that was very nearly a legitimately independent union, the workers balked at the proposed removal to the other side of the bargaining table from management. Moreover, when GE's workers were actually unionized a decade later (under subtle but potent prodding from management), the transformation was accomplished with a minimum of friction and without disruption of the workers' enthusiastic pride in being a part of the General Electric Company.

It was Owen Young, "Mr. Outside," whose function it was to create for himself and the corporation the image of the wise, kindly father figure. Young was one of the nation's most revered businessmen of the twenties, not because of the skill with which he ran his company (Swope ran the company) nor because of his identification with

the celebrated (though, as it turned out, calamitous) plans
for reorganizing payments of World War I reparations, but
because he hired the talents of some of the ablest practi-
tioners of the new art of public relations to manufacture
popularity for him. Bruce Barton, soon to move somewhat upward by publicizing Jesus Christ as the first modern businessman, was Young's original hired tout: Barton
created a public image of Young (and incidentally of GE)
as the corporate executive (and incidentally the corporation) with a heart, as the man and the company who put
service to the public first and profits a distant and relatively
insignificant second. ("At General Electric, Progress is
our most important product.") After Barton came Ida Tarbell, erstwhile muckraker, later more famous as a biographer of Lincoln, who in a commissioned biography made
Young into the Abe Lincoln of the corporations. Tarbell
carried the Lincoln parallel to extravagant lengths, depicting Young as a tall, lanky, homespun man of the prairies,
the man Lincoln would have been had he been so fortu-
nate as to have been born in more enlightened corporate
times. Capping her performance, Tarbell gushed that
Young was bringing "government of the people, by the
people, and for the people" to the corporation. As John
Fiorillo put it, "Who can argue with the Gettysburg Ad-
dress?"

Owen Young was not alone: he was merely one of the
more successful in a list of executives that included Henry
Ford and John J. Raskob, of corporations that included
American Tel & Tel, Du Pont, and Standard Oil, of
publicists that included Ivy Lee, Edward L. Bernays, and

91

Bernard Mullaney. In short, depicting the corporation and the corporate executive as public benefactor became all the rage. Together, such men and institutions glorified American business enterprise, created institutional as opposed to product advertising, and credited the corporate business community with all the chickens that were so abundantly coming into everyone's pot. But if you claim the credit for prosperity, you have also to assume responsibility for depression. To garble the metaphor, all those chickens would soon come home to roost.

The key figure in bringing them home to roost was Samuel Insull. Elsewhere I have attempted to capture Insull's career in a biography, and beyond making a couple of crucial points I shall not recapitulate that effort here. In general terms Insull was one of the most creative businessmen America has ever known: he was as instrumental in his particular field of endeavor, that of making electric power universally cheap and abundant, as Alexander Hamilton, John D. Rockefeller, and J. P. Morgan were in their special fields.

Insull was also—and at the same time—at least as successful in the field of employee relations as Swope was, and at least as successful in the area of public relations as Young was. More than three decades after Insull was forced to resign, in total disgrace, from the complex of companies he had created, I had occasion to interview several score of his former employees, and found them uniformly proud that they had once been associated with the man, if only as a lowly meter reader. In the broader area of public relations, Insull's impact was even greater. Building upon his experience as a propagandist for the

United States government during World War I, Insull
created an efficient and almost unbelievably well-organized
nationwide machinery for combating socialists and other
radical enemies of utility companies in the 1920s. So popular did Insull become that, when his New York bank creditors sought in 1932 to find an individual debenture holder
to bring the legal action that foreclosed Insull Utility Investments, they had to go all the way to Iowa to find one
who would do it; and that, when *Fortune* magazine sent
John T. Flynn to Chicago a few months later to write a
muckraking article about Insull, Flynn was astonished to
learn that virtually no one in the Middle West was willing
to condemn Insull himself, his companies, or his industry.

Insull was, to be sure, soon and decisively renounced:
he became the leading symbol of the depression and of
the evils of capitalism. On the face of things, it would
appear that his condemnation stemmed directly from the
fact that he lost, that his multibillion-dollar complex of
companies failed, and that he took his stockholders, more
than half a million strong, down with him. Actually, as
was demonstrated in 1962 by Arthur Taylor, then a gradu-
ate student at Brown University, now president of CBS,
only about 20 percent of Insull's securities went in default—and all of them at the upper levels of control where
Insull and his intimates had personally invested, none at
the operating company level—as against the approximately
40 percent default of all American corporate securities
during the Great Depression.

Insull's mistakes, in truth, and the failings by which
he brought upon corporate businessmen the wrath of public and politicians, lay in three separate areas. One was

93

that he and his organization, and especially his brother Martin Insull, offended the governor of New York, one Franklin Roosevelt. A second was that Insull was even more successful than Owen Young and Henry Ford and J. J. Raskob in creating an impression among the general public that corporate businessmen were public servants, as opposed to private citizens who like other private citizens had the right to work for their own private benefit. (Unfortunately for Insull, he believed and practiced what he preached: during his glory days of the late twenties, when his salaries of upward of $500,000 a year put him in the top ranks among corporate executives, he gave away more than he earned.)

Neither of these sins, however, was fatal. The fatal flaw was the third: Swope and Raskob and several other leading corporate executives upset the existing order of things, but none overtly challenged it. Insull did. In the depths of his being, Insull did not really care about making money, he cared about running things, and about running things in a way that was consistent with his notions of the public interest. To employ Hamiltonian terms, his consuming passion was ambition, not avarice—the love of power, not the love of money.

Ayn Rand, the high priestess of profit, would doubtless have disapproved of Insull, had she known what he was about; and the House of Morgan, committed to the proposition that the only reasonable aim in life is profit, both understood and disapproved. To comprehend what Morgan did in the economic crisis of 1931–32, it is crucial to know that there is a great deal of influence to be had and very little money to be made from the operation of public utilities. The source of the influence is obvious: utilities, by definition, supply indispensable transportation and motive power. But because they are natural monopolies (and thus necessarily regulated industries) utilities are capital-intensive businesses whose returns upon investment are fixed about at the prevailing cost of money, or rather slightly above that cost. If deposits in a savings account can earn 5 percent, utility corporations are allowed to earn no more than 5½ or 6 percent. Such steady but modest returns are not the stuff of which great fortunes are made.

The big money in utilities—in railroads in the era of the Vanderbilts, and in electric utilities in Insull's era—was to be made either in construction or in finance. Mr. Samuel Insull, Jr., has pointed out that the rule of thumb for measuring the legitimacy of a public utility holding company system in the 1920s was to ask who owned the construction company: if an individual owned it, the entire operation was run for private profit, and if the subsidiary operating companies owned it, the system was run for the benefit of the stockholders and the consuming public.

What neither Insull Sr. nor Insull Jr. entirely understood was the financial side of the operation: utility bonds afforded hidden opportunities for profits that dwarfed the visible profits of commissions on initial sales. For one thing, because utilities issued bonds regularly and in relatively large quantities—at an average of about 10 percent of a company's total capitalization every year—they made possible huge secondary market profits. The house that marketed the bonds of a particular utility had the exclusive function of protecting both buyer and issuer by "making a market" for the bonds: that is, trading them on the open market to stabilize their prices within a certain range.* Furthermore, it continued this function even when new issues were not being offered. Only small purchases were necessary: $50,000 daily might be all the trading in the bonds of a $100 million corporation. But over a period of time the bond house could accumulate large holdings at the bottom of the permitted range, do everyone a service by running the price up to the top of the range, and then sell its accumulated holdings to a single institutional buyer at the market price and thus at a sizable profit. Over the life of a bond issue, the investment bank that managed it could make as much in this manner as the entire face value of the issue. In addition, utility issues offered another special source of profit. Utilities were being consolidated as rapidly as they were being expanded, and with every reorganization it was necessary to call in all the securities issued before consolidation and issue new ones. Reorganization yielded a double commission on the total capitalization of the consolidating companies.

Back to Insull: Regarding money as only a means to an end, he never sought to understand the intricacies of the bond business, any more than he tried to learn the inner economics of the law firms or printing companies or other businesses that supplied him goods or services. Instead, he entrusted his bond business exclusively to the man who had for twenty years served him best, Harold Stuart

* This practice is now illegal but continues to be necessary. Investment bankers get around the law surreptitiously, but not so profitably as they once did.

of Halsey, Stuart and Company of Chicago. Through that connection, and by virtue of the fact that the New York banking community was preoccupied in the early twenties with international finance (Owen Young's other area of contribution to this story), Stuart became the dominant force in the utility bond business, which by the late twenties was reaching a volume of a billion dollars a year. In 1927 Harold M. Stanley, a new partner in the House of Morgan, convinced his associates that New York should take this lucrative business away from Chicago. The only way to get Stuart's financial business was to capture control of the utilities business of Samuel Insull. Capture it the House of Morgan did, in 1931–32.

I shall not burden you with the details of how they did it; that is not especially relevant here. What is relevant is that the New York financial community, after successfully pulling off an act of plunder that involved more money than the Spaniards took from the Aztecs and the Incas combined, covered its crime by framing Insull—by juggling the books and changing the accounting system in such a way as to make Insull appear retroactively to have been a crook. Not satisfied with that, Mr. Owen D. Young, having previously become chairman of the New York Federal Reserve Bank and a thoroughgoing Morgan man, lent his great prestige to the plunder by serving as the head of the bankers' committee that foreclosed Middle West Utilities, Insull's major holding company, and subsequently testified before Congress that the Insull system was so complex that nobody could possibly understand it. (The Insull system was so simple, in fact, that even I was able to understand it thirty years later: all that

97

was involved was a regional system of organization, one major and several minor subsidiaries per system.) On top of Young's renunciation of Insull came a larger blast from inside the New York financial community: an article by Thomas Lamont, owner of *Collier's*, denouncing most utility operators and no small number of financiers—not including, of course, the House of Morgan, of which Lamont himself was a partner. After that, veritable hordes of businessmen got into the act, and the cry was always the same: "Sure, a lot of businessmen are crooks, but it's them, not us."

In sum, to cover its own misdeeds the House of Morgan set off what became an orgy of denunciations of businessmen by businessmen, at a time when solidarity in the business community was imperative to the very existence of the capitalistic system as it had so far been known. Other businessmen saw the merits of Morgan's position, and likewise began to denounce scapegoats for every evil, real and imagined. The only thing resembling a parallel in American history that I know of had taken place during the presidency of Ulysses S. Grant, when politicians indulged themselves in an orgy of whistle blowing on one another, thus discrediting their entire calling and, for nearly a generation, making it difficult for an honest or even a dishonest politician to make a decent living. The ramifications of the business world's venture into fouling its own nest were far greater.

FOR THE MOMENTUM THUS STARTED could not readily be stopped. Contrary to popular mythology, Franklin Roosevelt's New Deal did not begin with any special bias against business, large or small, except in regard to a handful of personal vendettas. As indicated, Roosevelt was personally hostile toward the Insulls, mainly as a result of a public debate in which Roosevelt had taken on Martin Insull and been thoroughly enraged by the younger Insull's superior knowledge and contemptuous, even insulting manner. The President also bore a grudge against a former friend, Howard Hopson, who had all but laughed at him when he sought (before deciding to resume his political career) an executive job with Hopson's Associated Gas & Electric empire. Except for such cases, however, in which he would seek vengeance, Roosevelt started out expecting and planning an administration based upon mutual cooperation with business.

The events inside the business community in 1932 and 1933, however, made the utility industry too good a political target to resist: after all, the bankers had delivered the utility people's heads on a platter. Accordingly, most of the genuinely radical permanent measures—as distinguished from temporary emergency measures—of the early New Deal were aimed totally or mainly at destroying utility companies: the Public Utility Holding Company Act of 1935, the acts creating the Securities and Exchange Commission, the Tennessee Valley Authority, and the Rural Electrification Administration, and significant portions of the Corporation Bankruptcy Act and the Wagner-Connery labor act.

For a time the New York financial community got off lightly. To be sure, President Charles Mitchell of the National City Bank went to jail for neglecting to pay his income taxes, but that was a flukish episode; and the president of the New York Stock Exchange, Richard Whitney, also went to jail, but that was the handiwork of the Republican district attorney, Thomas E. Dewey; and Chairman Albert Wiggin was forced out of the Chase National Bank, but he was allowed to take his ill-gotten gains with him. Most importantly, no significant punitive measures were taken—at first—against the banking community as a whole or against the Morgan group of New York bankers in particular. Indeed, no person in the Morgan group was indicted for anything, and no less a crusader than Ferdinand Pecora, chief counsel for the Senate subcommittee on banking and stock exchange practices, publicly commended the Morgan group for its integrity. (The Pecora committee, like congressional committees in our time, captured scores of headlines with sensational disclosures, but in fact never found out much of anything. At one point a disgruntled ex-partner of the Morgan firm tried to "tell all," but the truth was so far from the senators' preconceived notions that he was reprimanded for straying from the point.)

But the matter could not rest there: what New York started, Chicago and Cleveland finished. Harold Stuart and Cyrus Eaton—who had first become acquainted when Eaton attempted to muscle in on Insull utility financing, but became friends after Eaton courageously testified to the honor of both Stuart and Insull in their 1934 mail-fraud trial—had both been powerful investment bankers in 1929 and both were nearly broke by 1934. Both were also fairly young and determined to make a comeback. As it happened, Eaton was one of the few financiers who had direct access to the ear of the President. Eaton and Stuart put their heads together, and then Eaton called upon "that man in the White House" and told him how to break up the House of Morgan, clean up utility finance, and incidentally make it possible for Eaton and Stuart to get back into the game. Out of that interview came the legislation divorcing investment banking from commercial banking and requiring competitive bidding on the marketing of utility securities. That ended the client relationship between investment bankers and utility corporations, and finally broke the stranglehold that the House of Morgan had on the American economy. So in the end, everybody lost.

That is not quite accurate. If I may quote Samuel Insull, Jr., one more time, "Year after year and generation after generation, New York maintained its financial supremacy against all comers—Boston, Philadelphia, San Francisco, Cleveland, Chicago—until one day Washington won it all."

Chapter V

The Government as Godfather

IT IS EASY TO MISUNDERSTAND the presidency of Franklin Roosevelt. He was a vigorous leader in a time of grave national crisis, and as such he aroused deep emotions—both pro and con—that still have not fully subsided. He was an unphilosophical man, willing in the emergency to try anything that promised to work; he had in him much of the dilettante, and sometimes seemed more interested in amusing himself than in the consequences of his actions; often he was more concerned with political expediency than with substantive policy. Accordingly, his administration was marked by inconsistencies, tactical shifts, and what might be called palace revolutions, and it contained elements of socialism, fascism, and various other doctrines that defy categorization.

Nonetheless, there was direction in Roosevelt's administration—one we have followed ever since—even if he was never fully conscious of the course he was steering. That course can be described fairly simply. The primary drive in American life since the 1890s had been toward rationalization in the interest of order and efficiency; the humanitarian underpinnings of that drive were social control and paternalism. Nothing in Roosevelt's heritage or personal history or public experience qualified him to work very effectively in the area of rationalization; everything in his heritage, history, and experience dictated sympathy with social control and paternalism. Being a man of his times, he began his administration with a determined effort to reinvigorate both the drive toward rationalism and its industry-sponsored paternalistic counterpart. Only when that effort failed—or when he lost patience with it—did he find his true calling: to embrace anew the traditions of his social class, vigorously renounce business, and concentrate almost totally upon an effort to nationalize and politicize paternalism in America. The great corporations had unwittingly paved the way by teaching the common man to look to Wall Street instead of himself for salvation. Roosevelt's mission was to teach him to reject the false saviors on Wall Street and look to the true saviors in Washington.

In attacking business and encouraging paternalism, Roosevelt was sometimes denounced as a "traitor to his class," since he was a wealthy man. Nothing could be more remote from the truth. Roosevelt's class was the same as Bolingbroke's, that of the landed gentry—to whom paternalism and hostility toward business were equally vital parts of one's heritage. For centuries members of this class had never worked (except at philanthropy or in the public service), had never "gone into trade," and had regarded merchants, bankers, and manufacturers with hostility, contempt, and (as the moneygrubbers grew ever more wealthy and powerful) envy as well. The gentry's notion of an ideal world was an orderly one in which status was more or less fixed, the new rich were kept in check, and the lower orders were well taken care of—provided that they knew their place, stayed in it, and behaved with appropriate deference. Consciously or unconsciously, Roosevelt moved the United States toward that kind of social order.

In sum, what he was really doing was returning the Bolingbroke tradition to its ancient Tory moorings.

APART FROM THE ESSENTIALLY UNPLANNED ATTACKS on utilities and banks, a flurry of largely preventive measures originating in Congress, and emergency steps to restore a banking system that collapsed on the eve of Roosevelt's inauguration, the primary concern of the first New Deal was economic recovery. Toward that end, the President adopted three major policies that had in common only their historic association with the more illustrious of Roosevelt's Democratic predecessors. One was an effort to cut federal spending and balance the budget, the route to prosperity followed (in vain) by Jefferson, Jackson, Van Buren, and Cleveland. Another was inflation through currency manipulation, the means advocated by three-time-losing Democratic nominee William Jennings Bryan. The third was economic planning, or national mobilization to fight the Great Depression, in the same way that Woodrow Wilson's War Industries Board had mobilized the nation to fight the Great War. In the first two policies, Roosevelt quickly lost interest: he gave budget-balancing a good try but was unable to obtain the cooperation of Congress, and he devalued the dollar by 41 percent but gave up on currency manipulation when the experiment failed to work its promised magic immediately.

The fling at planning was embodied mainly in the NRA, created by the National Industrial Recovery Act of 1933. The origins of the NRA were various: the old War Industries Board, a plan for industrial recovery proposed by Gerard Swope, the corporativist system that Mussolini had put into practice in Italy, and suggestions from an assortment of amateur and professional economists. It was based on the interesting premise that the rationalization movement of the preceding three decades had not gone far enough—that the economy was suffering from overproduction, destructive competition, and a complete lack of planning. To rectify these supposed ills, every industry was requested to draw up "codes of fair practice," along the lines of a "blanket code" drawn up by the President, the objects being to fix uniform prices, wages, and working conditions, and to integrate each industry, through its trade association, into what was in effect a single whole. When each code was adopted and approved by the President it took on the force of law. Within a year five hundred codes had been adopted, some 23 million workers were under them, and more than 4 million workers had been reabsorbed into industry.

Whether because of or despite these various policies, the nation began to recover. Before the end of 1933 the emergency was over, and by the end of Roosevelt's first term unemployment had been cut nearly in half, prices and profits were being restored in both industry and agriculture, and most indices were pointing toward full recovery within another year or two. Given the severity of the economic catastrophe that had devastated every nation on earth, the American economy was demonstrating remarkable resiliency and strength.

But Franklin Roosevelt had already abandoned the policies that had facilitated—or at worst not seriously retarded —this recovery. The reasons were several and varied. For one thing, recovery had been top-heavy, which is to say that the biggest corporations recovered fastest, which in turn is to confirm that the strong are stronger than the weak. For another thing, a new spirit of collectivism spread over the nation during Roosevelt's first two years, affecting everything from movies and comic strips to best sellers and politics. For still another, in the spring of 1935 the Supreme Court ruled the NRA unconstitutional, and eight months later it struck down the NRA's agricultural counterpart, the AAA. For yet another, there was a presidential election coming up, and in the absence of reliable systems of polling public opinion Roosevelt overestimated the strength of highly vocal political extremists on both right and left.

A more potent force than all these, perhaps, lay in the President's own psyche. In his most celebrated campaign speech in 1932, Roosevelt had declared that "the day of the great promoter or the financial Titan, to whom we granted anything if only he would build, or develop, is over. Our task now . . . is the soberer, less dramatic business of administering resources and plants already in hand." The fact of the matter was, however, that the President's skill and tolerance regarding the sober business of administration was virtually nil, and his love of dramatic action was virtually unbounded. He craved the limelight, he craved action, and he craved immediate results. None of these cravings could be satisfied by slowly nursing the economy back to health, or by waiting for a system of wages and profits and markets to work its own gradual cure.

The craving for attention could be satisfied through the medium of the newly developed radio, whereby in his celebrated Fireside Chats he could, with his marvelously persuasive voice, explain (and take credit for) everything that was being done. In this role he was a smash hit, winning public confidence on a scale that would have made the corporate executives and their publicists of the twenties downright flops by comparison, and inviting the suggestion—which made liberals quake with rage—that Roosevelt's popularity was based upon nothing more than his seduction of the voters via radio. I make no such suggestion: indeed, I suggest things would have been much different had there been no more to it than that.

For Roosevelt's craving for action and immediate results wanted satisfaction, too, and therein lay the springs of change. Action and results to the President's liking came from such programs as the Civilian Conservation Corps, which had a quarter of a million young men off the unemployment rolls within three months of its creation in March of 1933, young men being provided with security and sense of purpose and a healthful outdoor life planting millions of trees and otherwise repairing the damage that rapacious Americans had done to Mother Nature—and all for a paltry expenditure of $140,736,000. Less to the President's liking was the Civil Works Administration; though the CWA offered work of sorts to no less than 3,597,000 people during 1933, at a cost of only $214 million, the work was of little value to the workers or the government, and the amount of private relief it afforded was negligible. But the principle seemed sound, especially as it was explained to the President by Harry Hopkins, head of the Federal Emergency Relief Administration: all that was wanting was more money. (Roosevelt was later asked why he relied on Hopkins so heavily. "Harry gets things done," the President replied. So might you or I if we were supplied with the kind of money that Hopkins would administer.)

The arguments for expanding public works programs were, in fact, powerfully persuasive, even in those days before Keynesian economics had become fashionable. For big corporations to absorb as many workers as even the CCC had done, an enormous increase in the volume of business would be necessary, and that could take years; and besides, corporations would swallow up inordinate amounts of the new business in profits and managerial salaries. As to where the government's money would come from, it could always be borrowed, now that the banking system was back on its feet, and now that Congress had rejected the President's efforts to balance the budget anyway. Moreover, it was clear that the big corporations were back in the chips (in 1933 the nation's 2500 largest corporations, those with assets of $10 million or more, had a combined net loss of $163 million, and in 1935 they had combined net profits of $4.3 billion, out of a total national income of $57 billion), and it seemed only fair that they be taxed to pick up the tab, since they were obviously not fulfilling their civic duty to provide jobs for everybody. Spurious as this logic might appear to anyone who had ever dealt with corporate account books, it seemed flawless to Roosevelt and Hopkins, neither of whom was burdened by any such experience.

In any event, Roosevelt proposed, a pork-barrel-minded Congress approved, and Hopkins was given principal responsibility for administering a vast program of public works, and the federal government opted thereby not to entrust recovery of the economy to the businessmen and farmers and workers who were its human essence. The CCC was expanded, the CWA was abandoned, and the Public Works Administration, the National Youth Administration, and the Works Progress Administration were created. Most of all, there was Hopkins' WPA, which in its eight-year lifetime spent $11 billion, employed 8 million people, and built 600,000 miles of highways and 125,000 public buildings.

Thus was born the idea of the crash program—which, like many another New Deal creation, was expanded, perverted, and institutionalized by Roosevelt's successors. The basic premise of the crash program mentality is that there is no problem so large that a few billion dollars of appropriations by the federal government will not solve it. During the war that was soon to come, crash programs brought about the production of 5000 airplanes a week, and also the production of an atomic bomb. In the forties after the war, crash programs were set in motion and ultimately resulted in the construction of scores of thousands of low-income public housing developments, for which our black citizens are eternally grateful. In the early fifties came a crash program of highway building which—as every motorist now happily acknowledges—ended traffic congestion once and for all time. In the late fifties came the National Defense Education Act, which eradicated the blight of ignorance from our land. In the sixties the creation of the National Council for the Humanities overcame what had long been an American failing, the lack of couth and culture. In the seventies President Nixon disavowed the whole business, but it had become so entrenched a part of the American way that his administration was spending more money on skyrockets than the Roosevelt administration had spent on creating jobs in eight years.

There was another, more subtle and more profound legacy of Roosevelt's decision to become the first of the big spenders. In the short run the New Deal spending programs preserved something that was cardinal to the American system of values, namely the work ethos. A dole, a handout, might have been offered to the unemployed, but Roosevelt and Hopkins—neither of whom had ever (as they say) met a payroll or earned his living by working for an organization that had to show a profit to stay alive—were determined to ensure that the workers' dignity and pride and sense of worth be preserved by providing that income remained directly conditional upon work. In that noble aim, they succeeded.

But there was, to quote the celebrated economist W. C. Fields, an Ethiopian in the fuel supply. As was hinted earlier, it was the great corporations who taught workers the first lessons of the dependency mentality: look to the company, for it will protect you and keep you, and may, if you are sufficiently loyal, give you one or two things you did not actually earn. The federal government, a decade later, undermined that message, showing by example that it was not the corporation but the government that was there when it was needed. It did not occur to many to recall the story of the witch doctors of the primitive tribe who stayed in power by teaching the tribesmen to scorn the sun and worship the moon, on the ground that the sun shone only during the daytime, whereas the moon furnished light at night, when it was needed. Indeed, the New Deal shamans, more subtile than primitive witch doctors or corporate public relations men had ever been, taught a different lesson to workers on relief: that the government was not doing the workers any unearned favors, but that workers had an inalienable *right* to employment.

That was among the most revolutionary concepts in the history of the United States to that point. Until then, at the very basis of American ideas of freedom was the idea that every man was entitled to the fruit of his own labor. That meant that he was free to sell his labor or to hire the labor of others, at whatever price was mutually agreeable, but in exchange for that freedom every man took his chances on survival. Bolingbroke, Jefferson, and Jackson had not believed in such a heartless system; they took care of their workers in bad times as well as good. But their workers, it should be recalled, were serfs or slaves.

THE NEXT STEP was to institutionalize the protection of the little fellow against the big fellow—which was most readily accomplished in the area of organized labor. For a variety of reasons, earlier efforts to organize and politicize American labor had been largely unsuccessful. In the nineteenth century workers had joined unions in good times but unions fell apart in bad, losing membership and drifting toward utopian politics. During the Progressive period, Samuel Gompers and his American Federation of Labor met considerable success, unionizing a total of around 5 million workers, but did so at the expense of rejecting industrywide unionization in favor of organizing only skilled craftsmen, by crafts, and of rejecting political activism, and especially ideologically oriented political activism, in favor of concentration upon getting "more" through collective bargaining. Then in the 1920s, mainly as a result of the effectiveness of welfare capitalism and company unions, the AFL's membership slipped from 5 million members to about 3 million.

When Franklin Roosevelt took office he was not especially sympathetic toward organized labor, for he failed to perceive its political potential. At the behest of Senator Robert Wagner of New York, an old friend, he did agree that the National Industrial Recovery Act should include a clause encouraging collective bargaining and establishing a National Labor Board to supervise it. When the Supreme Court struck down the NRA, Wagner persuaded the President to support the Wagner-Connery Act (passed July 5, 1935), which established the right of workers to join unions and to bargain collectively, outlawed various "unfair" labor practices by employers, and established the National Labor Relations Board to supervise relations between employers and unions. What was most important, the Wagner-Connery Act rigged the law in favor of unionization, especially by requiring that all employees join the union if a bare majority voted to do so.

The union leaders who moved most vigorously to take advantage of the new law were those who, under the leadership of John L. Lewis, had long championed unionization on industrial lines. At the national convention of the AFL late in 1935, Lewis urged that the traditionally craft-oriented AFL support an all-out drive for industrial unionization; Thomas McMahon of the textile workers' union and Sidney Hillman and David Dubinsky of the garment workers supported him, but they were outvoted decisively. On their own, they then formed the Committee for Industrial Organization—but the parent AFL disavowed it and suspended the participating unions. Two years later the committee formally seceded as the Congress of Industrial Organizations.

Meanwhile, CIO organizers had begun to move, swiftly and decisively. In June 1936 Lewis took on the nation's mightiest bastion of antiunionism, U. S. Steel, renting offices in downtown Pittsburgh and placing his United Mine Workers lieutenant, Philip Murray, in charge. For six months Murray's organizers scurried up and down the Monongahela enlisting recruits, and in the meantime Lewis ostentatiously gave money and rounded up voters in support of Roosevelt's campaign for reelection. Lewis expected, and soon got, a suitable return on this investment. "Is anyone fool enough to believe for one instant," he asked, "that we gave this money to Roosevelt because we were spellbound by his voice?"

As U. S. Steel braced itself for the impending attack,

the CIO hit elsewhere. On December 30, 1936, after winning minor strikes in three plants, several bands of General Motors workers at Flint, Michigan, went on a sit down strike: instead of walking out, they followed a tactic pioneered by the wobblies, members of a radical industrial union that had briefly flourished three decades before, and occupied the plant and held it for six weeks. Workers in other General Motors plants soon followed. Local police were unable to oust the workers, and Democratic governor Frank Murphy, a close ally of the President's, refused to call out the state militia to break the strike. Despite great pressures President Roosevelt also refused to act. In mid-February General Motors' management capitulated, recognizing the union and reopening under a union contract. A month later Benjamin Fairless of U. S. Steel surrendered without a fight: he signed a contract with the CIO Steel Workers Union, granting a wage increase and establishing a forty-hour week.

In the next six months the United Rubber Workers, through the use of similar tactics, had won a contract from Firestone; the Electrical and Radio Workers had won at General Electric, RCA, and Philco; and the textile workers had won at several major plants and increased their membership to 450,000. During the year there were no fewer than 4740 strikes and other work stoppages.

Then came a bizarre turn of events. A steep recession set in late in 1937, most factories closed or cut back production, and unemployment soared to more than 10 million. Historically, unemployment had killed unions, for workers were wont to betray one another in competition for jobs. The danger to the unionization movement in the winter of 1937–38 was particularly acute in the automobile industry: General Motors was drastically cutting back production and the CIO organizers had made no headway against Ford and had only a tenuous footing at Chrysler and the other smaller companies. But Harry Hopkins' Works Progress Administration came to the rescue, providing temporary relief work for the laid-off auto workers. Then the United Auto Workers, with surreptitious prodding from Hopkins, hit upon the audacious notion of organizing the WPA workers. In one dimension that gesture was almost absurd, for workers on relief could scarcely demand anything, and it was not legal to strike against the government, anyway. But the WPA workers' boss was sympathetic, and they did join the union, and that kept the spirit of unionization and the UAW itself alive until the recession passed. By the fall of 1938 large-scale production had been resumed and the union emerged stronger than ever. Two years later even Ford had been unionized.

It was not, of course, until after the war that industrial unionization was more or less completed. Despite the passage of the Taft-Hartley Act in 1947 and the subsequent enactment by many states of "right to work" laws (that is, to work without joining a union), unionization continued to expand until the mid-fifties. At that time it reached a saturation point—17 million union members, comprising only a third of the total nonagricultural work force but the vast majority of industrial workers—and growth stopped for a time. Thus labor in the major industries was thoroughly cartelized, even as the industries themselves had been for three or four decades.

Meanwhile, the New Deal had initiated and subsequent administrations had implemented two other kinds of institutionalized security for the noncorporate segments of the economy. One concerned the relationship between big business and small. In 1937 Roosevelt came to the shocking realization that most big industries were dominated by a few firms (Americans make that discovery about once a generation), and declared war on the evils of monopoly. Thurman Arnold, out of Georgia and Yale, was unleashed as a special agent of the Antitrust Division of the Justice Department to launch suits against General Electric, the Aluminum Corporation of America, Du Pont, General Motors, the A&P company, and other corporate giants. Simultaneously, steps were taken to protect and promote small, independent businessmen. To protect small merchandisers, "fair trade laws" (many of which are still on the books) prohibited retailers from making discounts on the sale of appliances and established minimum prices for many consumer items. What was in the long run more important, the Small Business Administration was created and empowered to make low-interest loans to small operators. By the mid-sixties this agency had so grown that it was making 12,000 loans amounting to half a billion dollars a year, and by the end of President Nixon's first term the number and amount of the loans had doubled. At least in part for that reason, the failure rate for small businesses has been cut by two thirds from its historically normal level, to about 40 per 10,000.

The other area of institutionalized security established

by the New Deal was the Social Security system, created in 1935 and now known as OASDI. The original plan was that the system should be an actuarially sound retirement annuity program—which is to say that employee payments, matched by a levy on employers, would be invested so that at the age of sixty-five the worker would have earned his monthly retirement checks. Things did not quite work out that way: the system became as perverted as the crash programs were. For one thing, the government's Social Security "trust fund" was invested in government bonds, which is another way of saying the government spent it and owed itself the money. For another, politicians were quick to learn that it was popular with the voters to increase Social Security benefits and to extend them to every manner of loser. As a result, the system evolved into a welfare program paid for out of current taxation—with a regressive tax that falls heaviest on the poor and is necessarily ever growing. Ultimately, if the program continues to expand the way it has been expanding, 100 percent of the population will be on Social Security and will be taxed at the rate of 120 percent of their incomes to support the system.

THE GOVERNMENT GIVETH, and the government taketh away; blessed be the name of the government. For some time, however, the New Dealers were able to preserve the illusion that there need be only giving, and no taking away. For the fiscal year ending June 30, 1936, Internal Revenue collections totaled only $3.5 billion, up less than half a billion since 1930, and yet during that year the federal government was carrying 867,000 full-time civilian employees (up 44 percent since 1930) and more than 4 million emergency public works employees (up 4 million since 1930). To be sure, the public debt nearly doubled, from $16 to $28 billion, but the additional interest expense amounted to only about $3 per capita per year, and inflation (a phenomenon much desired in the 1930s) would easily absorb that.

And what the government had to give was only beginning: in addition, there were a host of subsidies of one kind and another. Some of the subsidies were available to almost everyone: thus the Home Owners' Loan Corporation of 1933 and its successor the Federal Housing Administration (created in 1934) bailed out homeowners who could not meet their existing mortgage payments and also financed the purchase of new homes, and the creation of the United States Employment Service relieved the idle from the expense of paying private employment agencies to find them jobs. Farmers were treated to a host of special subsidies through the AAA, the Federal Farm Mortgage Corporation, the Commodity Credit Corporation, the Rural Electrification Administration, and the Farm Credit Administration. Even industry, or at least portions of it, was subsidized through such measures as the Vinson Naval Parity Act of 1934, providing for the construction of 100 warships and more than 1000 airplanes; and so, in a less obvious way, were bankers, for somebody made the profits from those federally guaranteed home and farm mortgages and, more especially, from the marketing of U.S. government bonds that were being issued to cover the expenditures that taxes did not cover.

Lest one suspect prematurely that the distribution of

118

federal largesse was other than uniform, or indeed that it involved a bit of boondoggling, let me plead that you shelve your suspicions until we take up the rise of the wheeler-dealer. For now, however, it is not beside the point to observe that the Roosevelt administration was not throwing public funds around indiscriminately, but was, rather, keeping at least one eye focused at all times upon its supporters among the electorate, potential as well as present. As to the potential, for example, it could scarcely have escaped the President's notice that all those millions being lavished upon industrial workers might conceivably induce a few workers to desert the Republican political machines to which they had long been loyal. Nor, it may be assumed, did the administration subsidize farmers in the wheat and corn and hog and dairy belts of the Middle West without noticing that farmers in that area had traditionally voted Republican.

But it is toward the traditionally Democratic areas that one would, without undue cynicism but with a proper allowance for human nature, expect the larger tide of federal funds to have flowed, and one's expectations would not be disappointed. The backbone of the Democratic party was the solid South—the eleven states of the erstwhile Confederacy and the four border states. Between them, these fifteen states cast nearly two thirds of the votes necessary to elect a President in any election, and controlled, by virtue of the seniority system, every important congressional committee. Indeed it can be taken as a maxim in American politics that whenever the Democratic party controls the White House the South controls the government. When that happens, the nation can expect (a) a great deal of Jeffersonian rhetoric and (b) a massive southward flow of federal funds.

Accordingly, it was toward the South that the money did pour from 1933 to 1940 and beyond. The South (which is to say the white South, for the votes of the black South, when allowed to be cast at all, went Republican) got its share and more of the general New Deal expenditures; compare, for example, the paltry federal outlays at the Boston and Brooklyn naval yards with the handsome shipbuilding contracts awarded to firms in Baltimore, Norfolk, Charleston, Mobile, New Orleans, and the Sabine-Neches area of Texas.

And there was more. Let us look, for example, at the Tennessee Valley Authority, which New Deal pundits heralded as being among the most enlightened projects of an enlightened age of reform. Obviously, all the federal expenditure in the project was money exacted by force, which is to say through taxation, from people in other parts of the country, for investment in (let us not forget it) the racist Democratic South, where roughly a third of the population was held in peonage. Less obvious were the tricks involved in the establishment of TVA. The ballyhoo had it that TVA was to rehabilitate an area that had decayed because of the neglect of heartless capitalism, and also that it was to teach electric companies how to run a unified power system by providing a "yardstick" by which to measure rates and standards of service. More than once, President Roosevelt praised TVA's accomplishments in his Fireside Chats. Less than once did he point out that development of the hydroelectric capacities of the Tennessee Valley had been delayed for fourteen years by the refusal of the federal government to permit utility companies to develop them; that most of the cost of TVA's development, the cost of servicing investment, was paid for by taxes levied on the rest of the country; or that the accounting system used by TVA to justify its rates formed the basis of the federal indictment of Samuel Insull in 1934, and was forbidden as fraudulent for utility companies by the Uniform System of Accounts imposed by the Federal Power Commission in 1938. Nor did TVA's later defenders point out that the economic growth rate of the area continued to be among the South's lowest.*

Other measures, ostensibly national in application, were given one twist or another to provide that Southerners received disproportionate benefits. Most of the funds appropriated to the Rural Electrification Administration, for example—$400 million in 1936, when Roosevelt created the agency by executive fiat, and many billions more later—went to the South, for well over half of the nation's unelectrified farms were in the area, and electric service from utility companies was already available to most farmers outside the South who were willing to pay for it. (The rural electric co-ops were still able to borrow money from the REA at 2 *percent interest* in 1973. No small number of them were lending it back to the government at upward of 6 percent.)

* TVA is, of course, a sacred cow. In 1964, when Barry Goldwater suggested that TVA should be sold to private enterprise, he set off a storm of outraged denunciation. Actually TVA had been "sold," in effect, by the Eisenhower administration a decade earlier—that is, it was required to finance itself thereafter by the sale of its own bonds to private investors, though it continued to be operated by a government commission. In the 1970s TVA has been trying to get back under the government's wing, but to no avail.

The diversion of funds toward the South came to be institutionalized, after a fashion, beginning in 1938, when Roosevelt discovered the Negro voter and made a deal. Only about a fourth of the nation's blacks lived outside the South, but in several large northern states they constituted the balance of power in any election, and they voted overwhelmingly Republican. In 1938, to win them over, Roosevelt instituted a series of grandstand plays, most notably the proposal of a federal antilynch law. Such measures seemed harmless, for they changed nothing, but they aroused violent emotions among southern whites, and to ensure continued support of southern congressmen for his other activities, the President made an arrangement which most of his Democratic successors have honored. Publicly, the President would talk as a staunch advocate of civil rights, and the southern congressmen would denounce him vehemently; privately, the Southerners would support him on foreign affairs and domestic spending programs and the President would support them in continued efforts to channel federal funds southward.

The provisions of the revised Agricultural Adjustment Act of 1938 illustrate the nature of the bargain. The original AAA of 1933 had been ruled unconstitutional, and its ruthless policies of "plowing under" little pigs when people were hungry had been unpopular with the culturally conservative southern farmers. Interim measures enacted in 1936 and 1937 proved ineffective. The 1938 AAA was designed to and did raise farm prices and farmer profits through a complex subsidy system. The Secretary of Agriculture fixed production quotas which, after approval by a referendum of farmers, controlled the amount each farmer could plant. If production still exceeded what the market could absorb at "parity" prices (parity being defined as the ratio that farm prices bore to what farmers had to pay for nonfarm goods in the halcyon period 1909–14), the Commodity Credit Corporation took the surplus off the market by making loans to farmers against their crops at a price near parity and storing the unmarketable surplus. In times of shortage, the Commodity Credit Corporation was to sell its stored surpluses and write off the debts. That system worked with dramatic effectiveness to drive farm prices upward. Three of the five principal crops it supported—cotton, rice, and tobacco—were grown primarily or exclusively in the South.

With various modifications, the farm subsidy system is still with us—vastly expanded but as political as ever. In 1972 the Nixon administration, as a part of its overkill campaign strategy, paid out more than $4 billion in price-support subsidies, all the while talking a good antiinflation game. The system, of course, favors the incumbent: the hapless McGovern repeatedly claimed that he had done more to raise wheat prices over the years than anyone else, but the farmers knew who, just now, was laying on the loot.

AND YET, though political gain was the immediate motivation behind most of what the New Deal was doing—and though political rhetoric, as always, disguised what was happening—a distinct pattern was emerging by the time Roosevelt was sworn in for his unprecedented third term in 1941. Everybody from the President to the lowliest piney-woods redneck assumed that the bountifulness of

123

America was unlimited, and that somebody had messed up the system. The President and his economic advisors went further, believing that the great industrial corporations (like the railroads before them) were at once wicked and an indestructible cornucopia, and believing also that the only problem was one of maldistribution (or "underconsumption") of what everyone agreed was boundless wealth.

It was this gross (if entirely human) misconception, rather than a conversion to Keynesian or other new economic theories, that underlay the major changes adopted by the Roosevelt administration. Why not impose progressive taxes upon business and the rich, why not create a useless federal bureaucracy, why not impose unionization, inflate farm prices, vote endless subsidies? Couldn't the richest country in the world afford it?

Nor was it a concern for economic theory that gave the programs their general direction, for the underlying drive was social, not economic. That is to say, the concern was not so much for redistributing income as a means of energizing the economy as it was for giving everyone a sense of security. Failure was to be made virtually impossible, even for the weakest and least fit: most segments of society were to be guaranteed a floor, a minimum level of security beneath which the whole society would not allow them to fall. The opposite side of the same coin was that virtually every member of society was locked into his existing relative position, though having the illusion of upward mobility.

It would be quite some time before this fact would become visible, but it was an inescapable part of the New

Deal programs. What it meant was that neither equality nor equality of opportunity was to prevail in future: most members of society would go through life with the same relative status with which they began, being able to improve their lots only as the general lot of the whole society was improved, and all the while thinking they were rising.

Chapter VI

Wheeler-Dealers
and Unequal Partners

THERE WAS ONE MAJOR EXCEPTION to the New Deal's fixed system of status, and strangely enough that was in the area of business enterprise. Partly by accident, partly by design, the federal government's policies made possible the rise of the "wheeler-dealer"—the politically oriented businessman who makes enormous fortunes and gains great prestige and power by going into partnership with government, by exploiting special influence or inside information, or by turning to personal advantage programs that are designed for purposes of the general welfare. Ironically, however, it was in precisely this area that it first began to be apparent that the Americans had fixed themselves to a course that could end in paralysis.

A partial disclaimer should be made at the outset, for a considerable portion of what might be thought of as wheeling and dealing that took place in the 1930s and afterward was actually quite traditional, and was small potatoes as well. Patronage and the purchase of political influence had been part of the English and American political system since the eighteenth century; and though the scale grew larger during Roosevelt's presidency, nothing fundamental in American life was changed as a result. Thus, for example, when it was arranged that the President's son Elliott should receive a personal loan of $200,000 from John A. Hartford, whose A&P company was under an antitrust suit, it was no especial loss to the public that the pressure on A&P was subsequently relieved. Similarly, it was no skin off the backs of anybody in particular when a government loan of $1,250,000 was made to an Alaska mining company that promised a job to the President's brother-in-law, G. Hall Roosevelt; indeed, that operation was probably a public boon because it removed Hall Roosevelt as a nuisance who had the unfortunate habit of making personal business calls on the White House telephone.

Likewise, though some handsome fortunes were made by private contractors engaged in public construction, there was little that was new and nothing that was surprising about that fact. To be sure, the magnitude was greater than ever before, the federal government was now spending as much on construction as were state and municipal governments, and Democratic construction companies were getting more business than Republican companies. But the graft rate—the markup on what governments have to pay over what private industry would be charged for similar building—held steady in most places at an "honest"

15 to 20 percent during the 1930s. In due course, such solidly Democratic firms as Brown and Root, Campanelli and Cardi, and Perini Brothers would rank among the largest construction companies in the world, and would owe their success as much to their politics as to their engineering skill and efficiency; still, no basic changes in the economy or in the relations between government and business followed as a result.

Two kinds of qualitative changes did come about in the 1930s, however, one as a direct result of government activity, the other as a result of the operations of shrewd businessmen who took advantage of government policies that were aimed in a different direction. One example apiece should make each form clear.

By far the most spectacular operator in Roosevelt's government, in direct dealings with business, was the Texan Jesse Jones, head of the Reconstruction Finance Corporation. Though Jones and his agency were ultimately responsible for bringing about a catastrophic alliance between government and business, there was nothing inherently unsound in the idea of the RFC and he personally was a conscientious public servant. He knew how to get things done, he ran his powerful agency on a businesslike basis, and in doing his job he was scrupulously attentive to the interests of the public. He headed the RFC pretty much the way Alexander Hamilton might have done; and to anyone who truly understands Hamilton, that will be regarded as the highest possible praise.

But there were by-products—or perhaps necessary evils —attendant upon Jones's doings, even as there were upon Hamilton's. Jones had scarcely taken control of the RFC in 1933 when he realized that many crucial big businesses needed saving from their management as badly as they needed saving from their situations. In 1932, when he was a member but not the chairman, the RFC had aided troubled businesses only by making loans against good collateral. As chairman after 1933, with congressional authorization, Jones instituted a policy of buying preferred stock—*voting* preferred stock—instead. Thereafter, when the RFC rescued a bank or a railroad, Jones was able to dictate who management should be, and to fix management's salaries as well. Usually, the old management was kept on, albeit at reduced salaries and with a Jones appointee on the board of directors to keep everybody honest. Fairly often, however, Jones forced a new president upon the recipients of RFC funds. Occasionally, when that happened, the new chief officer was chosen as much for political as for business reasons.

A case in point is that of the Continental Illinois National Bank and Trust Company of Chicago. The Continental had been put together by George and Arthur Reynolds, brothers from Iowa who were more gifted in creating financial empires than in operating sound financial institutions. Through their inept management, especially in regard to the Insull collapse, the Continental got itself illegally and perilously overextended. The activities of a tough and able vice-president named Abner Stilwell kept the bank from going all the way under, but by the spring of 1933 it was, nonetheless, in serious trouble.

If ever action by the RFC was justified, this was it. On the one hand, the Continental was fundamentally quite sound, despite its difficulties; on the other, it was the biggest correspondent bank in the nation, serving as the city banking agency for hundreds of small "country banks," and its collapse would have precipitated a devastating wave of failures in its wake. The Continental's officers asked the RFC for a loan of $50 million, which was in fact a bit more than they needed. Instead, the RFC offered to buy $50 million in voting preferred stock, but only on condition that the bank "write down" its existing $75 million in common stock to $25 million—thus giving the RFC controlling interest in the bank. Reluctantly, but necessarily, the directors accepted the offer.

Sometimes, in such circumstances, Jones was able to place the best available man in charge—as he did in making Charles T. Fisher, of the Fisher Body Works, president of the National Bank of Detroit despite Roosevelt's fear that to do so might alienate industrial workers. In the case of the Continental Illinois, however, as in several other instances, Jones had to bow to the expediencies of politics.

Now observe, if you will, how the expediencies of politics unfold. There was a gentleman named William H. Woodin, who owned a company called American Car and Foundry and who happened also to be a Republican who deserted his party in 1932 to support Franklin Roosevelt. There was another gentleman named Walter J. Cummings, who happened to own a company called Cummings Car and Coach and who happened also, as an Irish Catholic, to be a lifelong Democrat. Mr. Woodin had a burning desire to acquire the Cummings company, and Mr. Cummings had a burning desire to be president of a big-city bank, as a means of attaining social respectability. Both gentlemen contributed heavily to Franklin Roosevelt's presidential campaign in 1932. Subsequently Mr. Roosevelt appointed Mr. Woodin Secretary of the Treasury, Mr. Cummings sold his company to Mr. Woodin and became Assistant Secretary of the Treasury, and Mr. Woodin looked around for a bank to make Mr. Cummings president of. Enter the Continental Illinois National Bank and Trust Company, Mr. Jesse Jones looking for a president of same, and the RFC, of which Mr. Woodin was by law a member of the board. *Voilà!* Walter J. Cummings became president of the Continental, and everybody was happy.

There was one little problem. Mr. Cummings was by no means a dummy, indeed in some respects he was an astute man, but he knew not the first thing about how to run a bank. Despite the excellence of his subordinates and the cushion provided by the RFC's investment, the Continental might soon have floundered again but for a fiscal innovation that somebody thought up. The New Deal was spending gradually but steadily more than it was collecting in taxes, and doing so in a novel fashion. During Roosevelt's first term the amount of outstanding U.S. government bonds—long-term obligations—increased less than 30 percent, from around $14 billion to $18 billion. The amount of outstanding treasury bills and notes —short-term obligations—nearly quadrupled, from $4 billion to $14 billion. Certain forms of treasury bills bore only moderate interest but could be used by the purchasing banks in lieu of cash for deposit reserves, and thus enabled banks to earn money on such deposits; moreover, such bills could be discounted at federal reserve banks as a basis of currency loans. Had all banks been able to buy treasury bills at will, the Federal Reserve System could have become infinitely fouled up. Instead, for practical purposes, a few "pet banks" were given the privilege of dealing in the bills, and all made a bundle. The Continental, it hardly needs be added, was one of the pet banks. Consequently, as Abner Stilwell put it, "the Continental made more money than it had ever made before, even though Walter Cummings didn't know his head from a hole in the ground about banking."

There is nothing especially inimical to the public interest in such doings—at first. If government policy regarding both business and fiscal management dictates a particular action, no harm is done if various individuals or institutions make inordinate profits as a result of the action. The danger comes later, after great fortunes have thus been made, for the politically rich obtain a powerful vested interest in continuing the policy even after it becomes obsolete. Their interest and influence constitute a barrier to change that is almost impossible to overcome. In this specific instance, government policy was aimed at stimulating inflation by loosening the supply of currency, an objective that was entirely desirable under the conditions that prevailed in the mid-1930s. By the mid-forties, when inflation had become a menace rather than a desideratum, government found it difficult to reverse the policy because too many powerful interests had too big a stake in the now established way. Instead, therefore, inflationary monetary policies were continued, and inflation was checked only by the imposition of new controls through the Office of Price Administration.

So much for boondoggling that locks up policy when government is doing favors for business. The same thing could and did happen in reverse, when vested interests were created in the continuation of government attacks on business. The game of making money out of government enmity to business is complex. In this peculiar form of enterprise, the most skillful player I have ever encountered is Mr. Cyrus Eaton. In his youth Eaton, a native of Nova Scotia, aspired to be a Presbyterian minister and was working his way through theological seminary by doing odd jobs arranged by his uncle, a lawyer in the employ of John D. Rockefeller. Rockefeller's wife, a religious woman, met young Eaton by chance and placed him as a summertime office boy to her husband. Rockefeller, a religious man, was impressed by the youngster's business abilities and convinced him that the work of the Lord could be more efficaciously done by people with money than by paupers. Upon Eaton's graduation Rockefeller assigned him to superintend construction of an electric power plant to service a refinery that Rockefeller's Standard Oil Company proposed to build in Manitoba. The panic of 1907 killed Standard Oil's plan for the refinery, but Eaton (then twenty-one years old) convinced Rockefeller that the investment in the electric utility was sound, anyway. The Great Man lent the boy $1 million in cash to complete the project on his own, and the boy was on his way. By 1929 Eaton (now a boy of forty-three) controlled $2 billion in utility properties. His role in the Insull collapse and in the banking legislation of the early 1930s has already been mentioned. By 1935, after tangling with

Wall Street in a number of misadventures, he was virtually broke.

In that year Congress passed the Wheeler-Rayburn Act, otherwise known as the Public Utility Holding Company Act. Several congressmen, including Senators Norris, Wheeler, and others, shared with the President personal grudges against various giants of the utility holding company world, and the Wheeler-Rayburn Act reflected that hostility. The most important section of the act was the famous "death sentence" clause, which required holding companies to divest themselves of all properties which were more than three levels removed from operating companies (holding company A owns holding company B which owns your local electric utility company), and also to divest themselves of all but a single "integrated" utility operation.

In some respects the legislation ran counter to the reformers' intentions. The system most directly and immediately hit by it was the North American Company, which Mr. Roosevelt had recently praised as "the Ivory Soap of the Holding Companies—99 and 44/100ths percent pure." Most holding company systems were spread over large territories but in one or two contiguous areas. North American happened to be a company that had developed utilities from cities outward toward suburbs and surrounding communities, in such widely scattered places as Detroit, Milwaukee, St. Louis, San Antonio, Los Angeles, and elsewhere. It was therefore, of all the holding companies, the least qualified to take serious steps toward becoming a single integrated property.

But there was a loophole, of sorts. North American,

like every other utility holding company system, had expanded vertically as well as horizontally—that is, had bought coal companies, barge companies, small railroads, pipeline companies, and the like, in order to reduce the costs of primary materials. The Wheeler-Rayburn Act decreed that holding companies be required to strip themselves horizontally as well as vertically—but not overnight. formers' intentions. The system most directly and imme-Instead, the Securities and Exchange Commission was vested with supervisory power over the divestment proceedings, the provision being that utility holding companies must forthwith show "good faith" by divesting themselves of holdings that stood in the way of progress toward the ideal of single integrated utility properties.

A gentleman named Harrison Williams, a man then so rich from financial and construction contracts that he could almost have bought Henry Ford himself, owned a Cleveland-based corporation called the New Empire Company, which in turn owned the North American Company, which (as indicated) owned the utility properties in Detroit, Milwaukee, St. Louis, and so on. The law said he had to start getting rid of properties; his lawyers told him to dispose of a few cats and dogs as sops to the SEC, thus buying time until the legislation could be changed.

As things happened, down Cleveland's Terminal Tower from Williams resided the nearly bankrupt financial operator Cyrus Eaton. What transpired between Eaton and Williams is known only to the gods. Eaton told me one version, *Forbes* magazine reported another, and the *Wall Street Journal* has told the story several ways. The consensus is the following:

One of North American's subsidiaries was the West

Kentucky Coal Company, which happened to be the largest nonunionized mine in the country. Eaton asked Williams for an option to buy the company for $5 million; this was rather less than it was worth, but the offer appealed to Williams as a ready means of relieving the political and legal pressure on him, and he gave Eaton the option. Eaton then entrained to West Virginia to consult his old friend John L. Lewis, president of the United Mine Workers, with whom he shared a passion for (you guessed it) ancient Greek poetry. After reciting a few stanzas, Eaton asked Lewis who controlled the Mine Workers' pension funds. After reciting a few laws and platitudes, Lewis allowed as how, in fact, *he* controlled the pension funds. Cyrus then asked John to lend him $5 million on a personal note at nominal interest. Knowing that a fellow Celt and fellow poet would not make such a request without ample motive, Lewis agreed to cause the UMW to make the loan. Forthwith, Eaton bought the West Kentucky Coal Company from Williams, the SEC got off Williams' back, Eaton refinanced the company and became a millionaire again, and West Kentucky Coal was unionized.

The first moral of this story is that individuals can become wealthy when government tears down an existing business enterprise, even as they can when government money creates a successful business. The second moral is more important: that negative policies as well as positive policies can result in the establishment of great political fortunes, and that these fortunes also make the policies well-nigh irreversible. I once met a lawyer who admitted to having made $10 million in legal fees as receiver of a defunct utility holding company. For some time the Honorable Dennis J. Roberts, former governor of Rhode Island, collected at least $50,000 per annum as one of three referees in bankruptcy for the New Haven Railroad. Given that kind of currency for paying and receiving political debts, there is absolutely no way that a defunct holding company or railroad will emerge from receivership or bankruptcy, or that the relevant laws and policies will be reversed.

Very well, you may be thinking: so what if a handful of people got rich by exploiting government policies, so long as the policies were adopted in the interests of the whole economy? The whole economy benefited; and certainly a random bank president, private operator, holding company receiver, and railroad trustee could not impose major limitations on the awesome power of the federal government, even assuming that a considerable number of government officials are corruptible by vested interests. I do not disagree, though I insist upon the principle: to the extent that government creates vested interests by implementing particular policies in particular ways, to that extent does government impair its ability to act flexibly in the public interest. Theoretically, at some point government policies can become so profitable to so many people that government loses the ability to change its policies at all—either because the interests it has created are too powerful to resist or because the economic disruptions inherent in a change of policy are too great to risk. Clearly, the United States had not reached such a stage when the peacetime New Deal ended in 1941. But the foundations had been laid, and the interests involved were about to become astronomical.

THE TAKEOFF toward the never-never land of the 1970s began with the outbreak of World War II. A great deal of what happened during the war can be dismissed lightly, at least for now. The huge growth of the federal bureaucracy, for example, was subsequently of portent—but not until later, and later shall we consider it. There was also a lot of busyness by an element that was then called "do-gooders" and what one of my current colleagues calls "the crazies." For example, Vice-President Henry A. Wallace had a notion, which was put into force under his direction as head of the Bureau of Economic Welfare, that efforts to harvest wild rubber in the Amazon region should be subordinated to a program of providing free vitaminized meals and social betterment for the natives of the area. (Wallace's efforts did produce some rubber, at an average of $546 per pound, which was only about 1760 times as high as the average wartime procurement price of 31 cents a pound.)

Most of the wartime production, of course, was turned out by well-established great corporations—by the likes of General Motors, Ford, General Electric, U. S. Steel, and Du Pont—and was facilitated by the larger railroad, mining, and electric utility companies. The officers and directors of such companies were plagued by old-fashioned hang-ups, long before "hang-up" entered the dictionary. On the one hand, they were patriots, people who loved their country and were willing to make any sacrifices necessary to its survival. On the other, though they had been castigated for three years as enemies of the people and bombarded for twenty years before that by company propaganda telling them they must be servants of the people, it was understood all along that they must also make a profit in order to survive.

In wartime, public service and profits were not entirely reconcilable. Automotive companies, for example, could produce vast numbers of tanks or planes instead of cars, but not at a profit, for conversion from the one product to the other entailed inordinate capital investment that would become useless as soon as the war ended. The federal government, following the characteristic American practice of adopting patchwork solutions, induced them to produce war goods by granting fast-depreciation write-offs against income taxes, and then levied excess-profits taxes to make sure they made no more money than was normal. When it was necessary to build and operate new and exclusively military plants (as opposed to temporarily converting peacetime plants) the government normally resorted to "cost plus" contracts—contracts which reimbursed the producer for all his costs and paid him an additional sum, a specified percentage of his costs, as a guaranteed profit. All in all, it was a fairly equitable system, though it had this interesting side effect, which the return of peace did not alter: the companies which made the greatest profits were not those who performed most efficiently, but those which had the best lobbyists and the best accountants.

The agency most important in bringing about this state of affairs was the Reconstruction Finance Corporation, for the RFC was at the center of a plan to shift control over production from private industry to the federal government. During the First World War, the government had invested only about $600 million in new industrial facilities, mainly in shipping, powder plants, and chemical plants; the remaining nine tenths of the plant expansion for the war was financed privately. An act of Congress passed on June 25, 1940—three days after the fall of France—portended the revised method that would be used in the second war. The RFC was authorized to purchase, lease, or build plants in any way the agency thought feasible, and in the next five years it built new plants costing $8 billion, increasing the nation's total investment in heavy industry by more than a third. By that means the federal government came to own 96 percent of the country's synthetic rubber industry, 90 percent of its magnesium metal industry, 71 percent of its aircraft manufacturing, 58 percent of its aluminum manufacturing, and dominant interests in the shipping, machine tool, and various lesser industries.

The process by which this took place is worthy of careful notice. Scrutiny of any industry would do, but the aluminum industry is perhaps most enlightening, because it illustrates so many different aspects of the elements that were at work.

When the war began aluminum was produced only by the Aluminum Company of America (Alcoa) and its subsidiary, the Aluminum Company of Canada. Alcoa had been founded and run since its inception by Arthur V. Davis, and had become a corporate giant through Davis' great ability, with the help of investment capital supplied by Andrew W. Mellon. In 1938 it was hit with a suit for violation of the antitrust laws. In 1941, with that suit still pending, Jesse Jones asked Davis to build a number of new aluminum plants for the government, operate them, and sell the government the product, retaining only 15 percent of the net profits as Alcoa's fee for thus competing with itself. Since Davis was the only man in the world who was capable of producing aluminum economically and in quantity—or, in any event, since Alcoa was the only company capable of doing so—Davis might have driven a hard bargain. But he was an honorable and patriotic man, and he acceded to Jones's request. Subsequently, he made the government privy to all the processes necessary to the successful and profitable manufacture of his product.

Shortly afterward, the RFC lent $16 million to a small but staunchly Democratic organization in Richmond, Virginia, known as the Reynolds Metals Company, for the purpose of going into the manufacture of aluminum, using Alcoa's patents and processes. Much larger loans were soon forthcoming.

Meanwhile, another staunch Democrat named Henry J. Kaiser was busily engaged in the building of ships in New Orleans and on the Pacific coast, with subsidies from the Federal Maritime Commission. Kaiser was heralded as a supergenius of production, for he was able to build his famed Victory Ships in sixty days; the fact of the matter was that his construction was extremely shoddy, and the merchant seaman who went on board a Victory Ship, even in harbor, did so at his mortal peril. But Kaiser was much beloved in Washington, and his campaign contributions were not notoriously miserly.

Kaiser was, through the great cost-plus ripoff, netting a profit of $60,000 to $110,000 on each of his ships, and now he moved on to grander things. Putting up a mere $100,000 of his own capital, he obtained a government loan of $28 million to enter the production of magnesium. Proving hopelessly inept at that venture, he moved upward, advancing another $100,000 of his own capital against an RFC loan of $110 million for the construction and operation of the Fontana steelworks. Fontana supplied ship plates and structural steel to the Kaiser shipbuilding firm at a handsome markup and profit to itself—and also increased Kaiser's shipbuilding profits, since both organizations were operating on cost-plus contracts.

The profits of the combined undertakings were subject to wartime income and excess profits taxes of 90 percent, but the ingenious Mr. Kaiser had an answer to that problem. He negotiated arrangements whereby his shipbuilding profits could be set directly against his RFC loans— meaning that he was acquiring equity without paying any taxes at all. As Jones put it in his memoirs, had the war lasted six months longer, Kaiser would have repaid his loans in full out of untaxed profits.

By war's end he was able to move on to still larger things. The RFC had built aluminum plants costing well over $1 billion. It would have been denounced as "socialistic" had the government continued to own the plants in peacetime, but since Alcoa continued to be under antitrust suit it would have been "reactionary" to sell the plants to that company. One possible alternate buyer was Reynolds, and the other (for no reasons except his political influence and the fact that he was already into the distantly related business of magnesium production) was Henry Kaiser. The government-owed plants were sold through public bidding, and Reynolds and Kaiser got substantially all of them at far below their cost.

Having thus created two enormous industrial concerns by what was scarcely distinguishable from a gift, the government subsidized them even more in the postwar years. It happens that the aluminum business is one of two major industries (the other being electrochemicals) in which the cost of electric power is a significant portion of the total cost of manufacture. In, say, the automobile and textile industries the cost of electricity could be increased fiftyfold and the resulting increase in the over-all cost of production would be minuscule; but in aluminum production electricity accounts for a large part of the total cost. Now, after the war the Truman administration continued and vastly increased the development of government-owned power plants, expanding the Tennessee, Colorado, and Columbia River systems and proposing to take over all electric-power production in the country. Power from government-owned plants is sold far below the actual cost of producing it; when this fact is admitted at all, it is justified on the ground that it protects the farmer and other "little fellows" from the exorbitant rates of the predatory public utility companies. Actually, it is aluminum companies that consume most of the power produced by government-owned facilities, and it is they who profit most from it.

ONCE AGAIN: the unfortunate part of all these doings is not that Kaiser, Reynolds, and hordes of others made profits at public expense; that had been going on, albeit on a much smaller scale, since Alexander Hamilton was Secretary of the Treasury. The tragedy is, rather, that vested interests were established in the continuation of extraordinary policies and activities, and that the extraordinary was soon to evolve into the ordinary and even the normal.

In America, government policies once established are always difficult to undo. Instead, normally, the old policies are retained and new policies are grafted on top of them. In keeping with this habit, the atmosphere of wartime emergency, genuine in 1941–45, was made into a permanent characteristic of American life by the invention of the Cold War. When the Cold War began early in 1947, the bogey of the monolithic international Communist conspiracy was employed by the Truman administration merely as a means of making popularly palatable a series of entirely sensible but politically unsalable policies—incuding the arrest of Russia's imperialistic expansion in the Near East, bailing out a financially exhausted Great Britain, and revitalizing Europe through the Marshall Plan. But the bogey caught the popular fancy right away, and before long, in keeping with a norm in America, our politicians themselves began to believe in it, behave as if it were real, and thereby make it real. By that means the Cold War became a semipermanent fact, necessitating (or making possible) a high level of government expenditures for defense without (except in the "limited" Korean and Vietnamese conflicts) requiring resort to the messy business of hot war.

Consequently in 1950, before the outbreak of the Korean conflict, defense expenditures were still running half as high as they had during the first full year of World War II; in 1954, after Korea, defense expenditures leveled off at $47 billion, more than double the expenditures of 1942; and by 1973, after Vietnam and after a considerable *détente* with both major Communist powers, defense expenditures remained above $80 billion, approximately the level during the peak spending year of World War II. The skeptic would expect that something more than national security has been involved in all this spending, and the expectation would be well founded.

Broadly speaking, two other sets of forces have been and still are at work. One set concerns the older segments of the corporate portion of the economy, those whose *main* function is the production and distribution of peacetime goods—firms like General Motors, General Electric, Du Pont, U. S. Rubber, and so on. After the war these companies quickly reverted to their main lines of activity, but as the Cold War burgeoned they also returned to defense production, some at a level of 10 to 20 percent of their total volume of business. That is not much, proportionately, yet for all but the very biggest it can be the difference between a mediocre year and a bonanza year. For example, GE can have a disastrous year in the production of generators and appliances, but make up for everything by its sales of "space hardware" to the National Aeronautics and Space Administration; and Chrysler Corporation can lay a perfect egg in its Dodge and Plymouth automobiles but recoup its losses through profits on such defense contracts as the sale of tanks to the Army.

Two examples will suffice to illustrate the way the junior partnership with government paralyzes business. One is that General Electric and Westinghouse are forbidden by antitrust laws and by court injunctions to exchange technical information. In regard to washing machines and eggbeaters that prohibition is at worst merely nonsensical. In regard to working out the technical details of complex electronic systems for military aircraft, it is absurd, and at the very least necessitates a duplication of research investment that is quite costly to the taxpayer—whose taxes, by the way, subsidize 85 percent of all the technological and industrial research done in the United States.

The other example is that government security-clearance requirements necessarily apply to all persons who seek employment in industrial corporations which have significant contracts for defense production. Now, it is one thing to argue that the Atomic Energy Commission could have done without the services of the Rosenbergs or even of Robert Oppenheimer. It is quite another to go to the extravagant lengths that security checks went to during the 1950s, with the consequence that private industry was deprived of the services of physicists who had once, in their naïve innocence (or arrogant stupidity), signed a petition for one cause or another that the FBI now classified as a "Communist front" organization.

The significance of all this is that business steadily sacrificed its independence; to the extent that it became dependent upon government, it ceased to be what John Kenneth Galbraith and others have called a countervailing force. It could no longer challenge government labor policies or tax policies, for example, any more than it could challenge government security policies. Thus in 1962, when U. S. Steel sought to pass along the costs of a wage increase by increasing steel prices by $6 a ton, President Kennedy could use the government's power *as a consumer* to force a rollback of prices, and force Roger Blough of U. S. Steel to swallow some hard denunciation into the bargain.

But, along the way, government also sacrificed its own power as a countervailing force: it became caught up in its own web. The juicier examples are to be found in government's relations with great industries, but first let us deal with a simpler case, that of the lowly cotton farmer. Under the first AAA (1933) and the second (1938), and ever since, cotton farmers have been subsidized by a complicated mechanism. The farmers set limits on their own production, but if production still exceeds domestic requirements, they can store their cotton in bins of the Commodity Credit Corporation and receive loans against it at the "parity" price, or rather at a ratio of parity set by Congress. In practice this means that if the world market price of cotton is, say, 25 cents a pound, farmers can lend it to the government at, say, 35 cents a pound. That takes care of the farmer quite nicely, and it takes enough cotton off the market to rig the domestic price at 40 cents.

Enter the international cotton merchants, sulking. How, they asked government, can they buy cotton at 40 cents a pound and hope to sell it in international markets, where the price is 25 cents? Government does not undo the subsidy system; instead, it creates the differential marketing subsidy, whereby American merchants buy American cotton at 40 cents and sell it on world markets at 25 cents, and the government picks up the difference plus a reasonable profit to the cotton merchants. That takes care of the merchants quite nicely.

Enter the American cotton textile producer, sulking. How, they asked government, can they hope to compete with Japanese textile manufacturers when they have to pay 40 cents for American cotton while the Japanese are paying only 25 cents for the same cotton? Until John F. Kennedy became the first President in a century from a textile-manufacturing state, nobody much cared. Kennedy did care, and he set out to help the manufacturers. Neither he nor anyone else was willing to dismantle the whole Rube Goldberg mechanism, for to do so would mean the ruin of 200,000 marginal cotton growers, who with their families cast a tidy number of votes. But as many more votes were being cast in New England by marginal textile workers, and Kennedy moved to do something for them. He wrangled from Congress authority to adjust tariff rates, within limits, and he used that authority to adjust upward the tariff on imported cotton texiles. For good measure, he slapped quotas on textile imports. Supposedly that takes care of the textile manufacturers quite nicely.

It did not. Enter the trade deficit of the 1970s, sulking. Despite the Kennedy Round, Japanese textiles sell in the United States cheaper than do textiles produced in the United States. The deficit could easily be rectified by allowing American manufacturers to lay off excess workers and buy American raw materials at what they cost foreigners, but to do that would cost votes and also undermine forty years of governmental wisdom. Instead, President Nixon devalues the American dollar. That failing, he asks

Congress for a five-year grant of power to raise or lower tariffs *infinitely,* as a necessary weapon in the international trade war.

Government policy was irrational at nearly every step along the way, and every step was well-nigh irreversible as well as futile. About half the marginal cotton farmers failed anyway, with the result that scores of thousands of southern social misfits were disgorged into northern cities to seek work or welfare. The nineteen thousand or so large, efficient cotton growers mechanized their operations, throwing many more thousands off the land. The system as a whole limited cotton production, and in the summer of 1973—when everything else in the economy was going berserk as well—the United States suddenly found itself with a shortage of cotton, and prices soared from the previous record high of 45 cents a pound to nearly 90 cents. Still nobody proposed a change in the system: instead, restrictions were placed on cotton exports.

When the federal government gets itself locked into such policies regarding big industry, the results are even more bizarre. A well-known case is that of General Dynamics Corporation, a company that was political from the beginning. General Dynamics is a huge corporation, war-born, whose stock in trade from the beginning has been rather heavier on production for government than for those portions of the economy to whom efficiency and quality of production are meaningful. Within ten years after the end of the war, General Dynamics was doing a vast volume of business but not at a profit: it was producing its 880 and 990 transport jet airplanes at an annual loss of $425 million. What was government to do? It could not let the investment (or the prestige) which it had staked in General Dynamics go down the drain; to let General Dynamics fail would be to throw many thousands of voters out of their jobs and bring into question the entire program of defense procurement and government planning. Instead—according to no less a source than Dow Jones, publishers of the *Wall Street Journal* and the *National Observer*—government laid upon the company a host of contracts for the production of missiles, submarines, telephones, and building materials for the military establishment, all of which added up to some $2 billion, and more than absorbed the losses from the company's bungling efforts to make an honest dollar by efficiently producing an honest product that anyone honestly needed or wanted.

The dilemma to which such policies inevitably lead was epitomized by the twin problems imposed by the National Aeronautics and Space Administration and Lockheed Aircraft in 1971–72. NASA—a technological marvel directed toward executing a political grandstand play—admirably accomplished its mission, amusing the great unwashed by putting men on the moon, though something like a quarter of the people confessed to pollsters that they thought it a fake. Be that as it may, people became bored with the entertainment, and government started to scrap it. Scrapping it was difficult, for NASA had employed thousands of the nation's best engineering brains, who were so highly trained that they did not know how to do anything else. But engineers do not cast many votes, and the pressure of politics upon government was so strong that the phasing-down became reality. The highly trained engineers were allowed to retrain themselves as taxicab drivers in New York City.

Almost simultaneously, Lockheed careened toward bankruptcy, largely because of its ineptness in securing and fulfilling government aviation contracts. It was not so organized that it could reasonably be entrusted with the building of submarines and telephones, as General Dynamics had been. But tens of thousands of aircraft workers in the Pacific Northwest, together with their wives and the storekeepers they support, cast a lot of votes; and so, unlike NASA, Lockheed was not phased out or even allowed to slip into oblivion. The Nixon administration and the Democratic Congress came through with enough cash to keep Lockheed Aviation in business. The same amount of money would have put a dozen more men on the moon.

The moral of the story should be overwhelmingly obvious. Both NASA and Lockheed were useless, by any intelligent criterion of economics or the national interest, but intelligent criteria could not be employed. Politically and institutionally it was impossible to continue the one or to discontinue the other.

POLITICS HAS BEEN DESCRIBED as the art of the possible; what we have seen here is how politics can make intelligent action impossible. There are, of course, ways around politics. Or rather, there always have been. It may be that we are now so thoroughly the victims of our history that the ways around politics are even more cluttered with impassable barriers.

Chapter VII

The No-Fail Economy, or, Being Your Own Thing

THE UNITED STATES HAS, since the trauma of depression in the 1930s, developed an economic system whose first premise is that no one is to be allowed to fail, or at least not fail entirely. (The international counterpart of the system, inextricably locked into it, is that the United States has assumed responsibility for bearing most of the cost of military defense for the non-Communist world.) The no-fail system, based as it was on the cornucopia mentality, seemed to be a good idea when it was being formulated, and indeed for a quarter of a century it has worked—or at least it seems to have worked. Some of its less advantageous implications, however, are just now becoming visible.

For one thing, the cost has been high. The system involves punishing or weakening the healthy portions of the economy by making them responsible for carrying the unhealthy. One result has been an inexorable decline in the economic strength of the United States relative to the rest of the world. At the end of World War II Japan and Europe were devastated, and the United States had the only solidly functioning modern economy in the world; it had over half the world's industrial capacity and a large portion of the world's agricultural capacity as well. By the early 1970s Japan and Europe (in part because of American military and other subsidies) had emerged as powerful economic competitors of the United States, and as rivals for the planet's limited resources as well.

Another characteristic of the system is that it is incredibly wasteful, and there is no way to make it appreciably less so. It is wasteful because irresistible economic forces (and, what is no less important, social forces as well) impel us to consume more and more, and equally potent forces compel industry to produce more and more. We have powerful institutional machinery for increasing what economists call the aggregate demand—the society's total demand for goods and services—but we have no effective institutional machinery at all for reducing demand.*

The Honorable John Kenneth Galbraith, erstwhile Ambassador to India and the Pollyanna of the New Economics, has published a succession of treatises dealing with some of these matters, and has somehow managed to remain optimistic about it all. He believes that the enormous growth of government as a consumer has been healthy,

* Practically all economists believe that demand could be reduced by increasing taxes or lowering the money supply, but they are mistaken. See Chapter VIII, below.

for example, on the ground that that enables the federal government to ensure perpetual prosperity by manipulating the aggregate demand. As we have seen, however, government's flexibility is quite limited, since for practical purposes it cannot manipulate demand but only push it upward. Similarly, Galbraith mistakenly believes that the ruling elite of corporate business can manipulate consumer demand almost at will; but this, too, is a one-way street. It is easy enough to teach people to want things, but far more difficult to teach them not to want things. I should like to see the wizards of Madison Avenue attempt, for example, to con the masses into exchanging their color television sets for black and white, or to give up their cars (as long as there is even a faint hope of obtaining gasoline for them) and voluntarily return to walking or riding the bus.

As to those who do the manipulating—the managerial class that Galbraith calls the technostructure—the learned professor is even more egregiously in error. He quite properly maintains that the technostructure of the big corporations is largely self-governing and has superseded its archaic predecessors, the capitalist and the entrepreneur. This is scarcely news: ever since the creation of the first of the great oligopolistic manufacturing industries around the turn of the century, the bigger corporations have been increasingly self-financing. That is to say, their volume of sales in relation to capital requirements is so high—enabling them to gross in two to eleven months an amount equal to their total capital investment—that most of them can pay for expansion out of earnings, and are thus not dependent upon outside investors. To be sure, they resort to what amounts to forced investment: instead of paying earnings to stockholders, they reinvest earnings and from time to time pay the shareholders stock dividends rather than cash. The shareholders, for their part, are normally more interested in appreciation of their investments than in dividends, anyway—a preference that is stimulated and made permanent by income tax laws that take only 25 percent on "capital gains" and have ranged upward to as high as 91 percent on "income." Periodic changes in the tax laws since 1945 have altered these pressures in detail, but the over-all tendencies in big business are toward divorcing the corporation and its management from its owners and/or original promoters, and—what is more important for present purposes—toward forsaking profits and concentrating upon expansion for its own sake.

So far so good; but having eliminated maximization of profits as the motive that impels the technostructure, Galbraith goes on to ascribe to its successful members a drive to make the goals of their corporations, and indeed of society itself, "conform more closely to their own goals." The flaw in this otherwise excellent model is its lack of relation to reality. The no-fail economic system has had drastic effects on our motivational patterns, effects from which corporate management is not exempt. In some measure the shift is a matter of morality, for the work ethos is at the very heart of the American system of morality and the new economic order invites the question: if society is going to take care of you anyway, why work at all? Scores of thousands of young people, who have never known any other system and therefore take the present one for granted, have asked precisely that question, and nobody has answered it to their satisfaction.

The rest of us have undergone a subtle but profound shifting in our reasons for working. If the cultural anthropologists are right—and I believe they are, for their judgment squares with everything I know about human history—men are driven to compete with one another by one or more of three desires: for money or territory, for power, and for status. Often the three are interchangeable and sometimes they are indistinguishable; depending upon the determinants of the prevailing culture, one or another may be repressed and others may be exalted. We saw earlier that Western civilization long suppressed the money motive and fixed status from birth, thus channeling almost all human competitiveness into rivalry for power. In the southern United States, the drive for power ultimately choked the economic drive, and in the North the drive for money was dominant. The Civil War established the preeminence of the northern way. Tremendous economic expansion ensued as a result—but the urge for status and power could not remain subordinate in a free society. In the absence of a regularized and culturally sanctioned system for recognizing status, the very wealthy indulged themselves in orgies of what Thorstein Veblen called conspicuous consumption, flaunting mansions and private railroad cars as badges of *de facto* status. The tougher and more ambitious—from John D. Rockefeller to Samuel Insull—were driven by a love of power and saw money not as an end to be pursued but, as Damon Runyon said of gamblers, only as a necessary tool of their trade.

In recent years, as a result of the no-fail economic

system—and of its accompanying system of essentially fixed relative status—we have undergone a fundamental reshifting of the premiums our culture places on these three forces. Money is no longer the socially approved desideratum it once was: on the one hand we sneer at the pursuit of it, and on the other hand we take it for granted. From the assembly line to the executive suite, almost no one can be moved to work for mere money. The drive, rather, is to prove to one's peers that one is *above* mere money, as money is reckoned by one's peers. At the level of the workingman and among the middle classes in the suburbs, the name of the game is good old-fashioned conspicuous consumption. Part of this is obvious—that part having to do with the acquisition of otherwise useless things such as second and third cars, color televisions, powerboats, skimobiles, and air-conditioned cabins in the country. Another part is less so. An esteemed colleague of mine points out that, while many workers on the Detroit assembly lines get caught up in the game of acquiring things, and several tens of thousands play the variant form called getting a college education, many employ their affluence in being idle. That is to say, they bunk work on Mondays and Fridays, and are content to live within the tolerably comfortable means they can earn by working three days a week. I suggest, however, that this derives not from a love of leisure (most workers are bored silly on their four-day weekends), but is a subtle form of status seeking: the worker who can do it is justly admired by his peers, and therefore ranks a step above them.

At the upper middle levels the motive is the same but the game is different, for everybody is moving upward at the same relative rate. As a result, in this age of credit cards and 95 percent mortgages, quite large numbers of people in the piddling income range of $25,000 to $50,000 have moved into the status-symbol territory that was once reserved to the very rich. They have "democratized" and taken over management of most charitable work, and are the primary sponsors of cultural activity. They gather in exclusive watering places, the sybaritic pleasure palaces called country clubs. In the Grosse Pointes and the Bloomfield Hills of Michigan, and equivalents elsewhere, they build (for the less affluent to gawk at) veritable mansions in such profusion as to suggest that the homes were mass-produced, as in fact they nearly were.

That being the sad state of things, the upper members of the technostructure are thrown back on their wits to prove that they are above the crowd. The object is to demonstrate that they command great wealth—as if they were rich instead of merely making a lot of money. The most pretentious affect the posture of gentlemen by owning major athletic teams, thus emulating the Virginia gentlemen who raised race horses, the petty princes who backed jousting contests, and ultimately the Caesars who put on shows of lions eating Christians so as to amuse the rabble; but their crude pretense is readily exposed by the fact that such types expect to earn a profit from what they do. Mr. Henry Ford II moved the search for recognition of status several steps upward when he recently proposed a zillion-dollar plan to rehabilitate the defunct downtown area of Detroit; but the kudos he won by that grand gesture paled somewhat when it became public knowledge that the venture was to be financed by someone else's money.

The most extravagant example of the upper techno-structure's pathetic drive for status that I know of is to be seen in Chicago, where the most extravagant examples of everything are to be found. The chief executive of Sears, Roebuck & Company has caused his corporation to construct the tallest building in the world, a phallic symbol so enormous that it will make the monument to the father of his country, George Washington, seem a monument to impotence by comparison. The building is as worthless as my next-door neighbor's second skimobile. Indeed, it is more so, for if La Salle Street gossip is to be credited, Sears is finding it possible to fill the building only by abandoning the high standards of production from its suppliers that Julius Rosenwald made an integral part of Sears's tradition: suppliers are in effect bribed to rent space in the building by easing off on their quality controls.

What I am coming down to is this. What motivates mankind are the drives to *have* (money), to *do* (power), and to *be* (status). In America the drive to *have* has been turned into the drive to *be*. The drive to *do* has also been turned into the drive to *be*, even at the highest ranks of corporate power. That is what is wrong with Professor Galbraith's model: corporate executives do not want to *do* anything, exactly, so much as they want to *be* something, and to be *recognized* as being.

Now the urge to *be*, I submit, has been institutionalized along with everything else. We have invented a marvelous device for recognizing who is who, a device as perfect as the pecking order that hens establish in a chicken yard. We call this device bureaucracy.

BUREAUCRACY WAS NOT ALWAYS A CURSE: when it was reinvented in the late eighteenth century it was in fact a Great Leap Forward. Bureaucratization, in that context, meant rationalization and was appropriately enough a product of the so-called Age of Reason: it substituted a system of order and achievement for the existing scheme of administration, whereby records were kept indifferently if at all, and both procurement and promotion stemmed from influence, which in turn stemmed from power or court favor. The grand military successes of the French Revolutionary armies and of Napoleon's—coming only a generation after France had suffered defeat and disgrace during the Seven Years' War—were in large measure attributable to bureaucratization of the nation's armed forces. So efficacious was the invention, indeed, that France was all but able to subdue the world. It failed only because Britain had happened upon an even more efficacious institutional invention, that of money based upon debt.

The government of the United States began to be bureaucratized shortly after France's was, and at least partly in emulation of the French example. The Federalists, in establishing the government, followed the British example not only in monetizing the public debt but also in administering government on a lax and personal basis; but the Jeffersonians followed France's lead and reversed the Federalists on both counts. Systematized administration, line-budget appropriations, a hierarchical chain of responsi-

racy was replacing *ad hoc* administration and *laissez faire* in business.

And thus, quite in advance of the coming of the New Deal, "enlightened administration," to use Franklin Roosevelt's euphemism for bureaucracy, had become a norm in both business and government in America. The New Deal gave considerable stimulus to further bureaucratization: not counting employees on make-work projects, federal employment rose from 603,587 when Roosevelt took office to 1.4 million when he was inaugurated for his third term; and state and local government employment, exclusive of teachers, increased from 1.4 million to nearly 2 million in the same period. Significantly, too, private employment at the clerical, service, and lower managerial levels increased by 2.3 million in the 1930s while the number of persons employed in productive skilled and manual labor was declining by 100,000 and the net national product was falling by $300 million.

In other words, the number of bureaucratic workers was increasing rapidly while the actual amount of work, or at least of productive work, being done was remaining the same or even declining. A century late, Parkinson's Law finally caught up with the United States.

Let us see how the law works—for, if allowance be made for exaggeration, exceptions, and special historical circumstances, it does in fact work. A single man in a small office, whether in government or business, gets his work done or (in business, anyway) he loses his job. If he does his work well he may get a raise; but at some point he begins to think as much of prestige as he does of money, for, if either of these is to mean anything above

163

the level of mere subsistence, they must be interchangeable. In due course, given a combination of skill and luck, he gains the status of having a secretary to do his paper work for him. If his efficiency is not thereby increased, two people now do the work that one did before, and he ceases to advance. If the man and his secretary do more than the man did alone, however, he continues to advance (even though the unit cost of work may have risen), and in time he earns the prestige of taking on an assistant. But—and this is crucial—if he is given only one assistant, the assistant is likely to be regarded as an associate, or more or less as an equal; and so the original productive man, to ensure that he maximizes his prestige, holds out until he can get *two* assistants. The two are peers of one another, and therefore identifiably his inferiors. Then another factor enters into play: it takes another clerical person to keep up with the personnel records, reports, and correspondence files accumulated by the first four. Five people now do the work formerly done by one. Meanwhile, the secretaries and the assistants (by doing their jobs well) earn higher pay and, if their work is satisfactory, also earn secretaries and assistants in their turn. The process might be styled the law of the proliferation of subordinates: it is not so much that the proficient worker rises in a hierarchy (after all, he is still doing the same old things) as it is that he raises his *relative* position by creating, as it were, a lowerarchy. With variations, that is how administrative personnel, public and private, increased by nearly 4 million in the 1930s while the amount of productive work was not increasing at all.

That might have been that; by 1941 work had almost

increased to meet the supply of workers, and the process might have stopped. But then came American involvement in the Second World War. Suddenly there was more work than workers, and for four years, in spite of wheeler-dealers and a variety of aberrations resulting from the friction between the need for action and the bureaucrat's natural instinct to work through the channels of red tape, bureaucracy in America earned its keep.

But Parkinson's Law, or the law of the proliferation of subordinates, continued to operate after the war was over. Despite huge cutbacks attendant upon demobilization of the 12 million persons in the wartime armed forces, federal and state civilian employment in 1950 was about 6 million, up nearly 2 million over the level of 1940. Government bureaucracy was at a postwar nadir in 1950, and yet employment had fallen since 1945 by only a sixth while the actual work government was doing had fallen by two thirds. By 1971 civilian government employment had soared to 12.8 million. Ah, you may say: but that figure reflects the Vietnamese War. You will be wrong. Throughout that unhappy conflict the total civilian employment of the federal government remained between 2.3 and 2.7 million, as it had during the Korean War. What grew was nonwar bureaucracy, employment on the state and local levels, which accounted for the entire growth.

Let me repeat: when there is plenty of work to be done, bureaucracy effectively channels it; when there is not, bureaucracy creates it. When work needs to be done and is not done, heads roll. When unnecessary work is being manufactured, the Peter Principle comes into play.

Everyone, I assume, knows about the Peter Principle. It is that, in any hierarchy, nothing works well because people are continually promoted until they rise to their level of incompetence. A teacher, for example, may be promoted to assistant department head if he is especially competent as a teacher, even though the two functions require entirely different talents. If he is good enough at his new task he is in time made a department head, though that requires still different temperament and abilities. From there he rises to assistant principal, principal, assistant superintendent, superintendent, and so on, as long as he does each job with competence. Soon or late, he arrives at a job he cannot do, and he ceases to be promoted. He is not *demoted*, mind you, just not promoted any higher. He has reached his level of incompetence. At any given time, Peter goes on, most positions in a hierarchy will be filled by people who have reached their level of incompetence, and are therefore unable to do their jobs. (At that point, it might be added, they are likely to cast about for assistants who can do their jobs for them, and thus Parkinson's Law is given new stimulus from a fresh source.)

The Peter Principle, like Parkinson's Law, is of course a caricature of reality, but any perceptive person who has ever worked in a hierarchy recognizes that the caricature is nearly as accurate as it is humorous—and in some organizations a great deal more so.

It must be observed, however, that there are limitations upon the Peter Principle, imposed by the necessity to make ends meet. The principle admittedly runs amok in those areas in which (by one fluke or another of the interplay of institutions) the need to make ends meet is temporarily nonexistent. The most familiar of such flukish examples is doubtless that of education. After many decades of being ranked, in the public estimation, far behind such pressing necessities as giving bonuses to veterans, abolishing alcohol, and cleaning the streets, education suddenly came into public favor after 1957, when Sputnik I seemed to demonstrate that Russia had somehow sneaked ahead of the Americans in smarts. Appropriate crash programs were instituted, the National Defense Education Act was passed, and the country's institutions of higher learning were deluged with more money than they knew what to do with. Or rather, more than they would have known what to do with before Peter. The institution which employs me rose to the challenge by creating vice-presidencies and deanships at a staggering rate, until its ratio of administrators to students seemed to be approaching one to one, and my institution was not atypical.

Private business enterprise cannot work just that way, however: in business, though the urge to make a profit has been atrophied, the need to make ends meet is ever present, except (as we shall note when we get around to taxes) when it is not. In any event, business ordinarily needs to do somewhat better than break even, and that diverts—though it does not defeat—the working of the Peter Principle. What happens is that the inner logic and requirements of bureaucracy come to dictate what it is possible for an organization to do. Not supply and not demand, nor even technology or economics or government, but bureaucracy itself.

Perhaps I can illustrate this deflective influence by

reference to a business with which I have had some experience in several capacities, that of publishing books. When I worked at the State Historical Society of Wisconsin in the middle 1950s, the organization's publication division employed two female editors, who (except for the actual manufacturing) did all the work involved in publishing four or five books and four issues of a magazine per year. The combined salary of the two ladies was about $8500, which means that the administrative overhead cost of the publication program was (if we count four magazine issues as equal to one book) between $1400 and $1700 per title—or, in printings of 1000 copies, $1.40 to $1.70 per volume. Printing costs were about $2 per volume for a 300-page book on a press run of 1000, bringing the total cost to around $3.50. In those days it was reckoned that there was a psychological barrier to paying more than $5 for a historical monograph, and the market was small in any event; but, even so, the Historical Society could come fairly close to breaking even on its publications, given the simple administrative structure just described.

Across the street was the University of Wisconsin Press, where the workings of Parkinson's Law (though not, just yet, of the Peter Principle) were quite advanced. The administrative overhead of the press was $72,000, on which it published twenty-four titles a year—or a cost of $3000 per title, twice the Historical Society's cost.

Then came the hang-the-cost, no-price-is-too-high-to-pay-for-education 1960s. The press, operating at staggering deficits, grew until it was grossing around $1 million a year in sales. The Historical Society also expanded:

now it employs four people in its publication program (not counting secretaries who can occasionally be borrowed from other departments), at a combined annual salary around $60,000—and is *still* publishing four or five books and four issues of the magazine a year, now with an overhead around $12,000 per title, or $12 a volume on press runs of 1000. Nor, even in these days of budgetary stringency, is there any point in curtailing operations, for all the personnel involved are on civil service and would have to be paid anyway. The cost of manufacturing books, not having increased proportionately, has become a relatively small portion of the whole cost, and some of the overhead can be retrieved out of sales. Accordingly, it is cheaper for the state of Wisconsin to continue publishing at a loss than it would be to stop publishing at a loss.

In commercial publishing, bureaucratic overhead is so high as to dwarf that of scholarly presses, even though commercial houses can and do cut their payrolls in times of stringency. Let me offer two examples of the way the principle of bureaucratic deflection works with them. In the buoyant sixties, when the market for anything in print seemed infinite, overhead became nearly so. Some readers may remember the craze for publishing collections of historical documents. What underlay it was that it offered a means of cutting the overhead almost to nothing: a couple of historians would be hired as editors on a straight commission of, say, 7.5 percent of the gross, and they would subcontract with a historian who actually prepared the copy for a royalty of, say, 2.5 percent. These historical entrepreneurs produced manuscripts ready for the printer at almost no direct cost to the publisher. (The flaw in the scheme was that the books did not sell. I did such a volume in 1968, and it has not yet sold enough even to earn back my modest advance; indeed, for the last two years the royalty statements have shown *negative* sales, an excess of returns from bookstores over sales to them.)

The other example is what happened when the educational (and with it the publication) honeymoon ended in 1970 or 1971. It is a rule of thumb in commercial publishing that reducing costs by $1000 has roughly the same effect on the profit-and-loss statement as increasing sales by $15,000. When bad times set in, publishers understandably started slashing costs. But instead of firing administrative personnel, on the theory that the sales force must be retained to sell the supply of books already on hand, many publishers cut their *sales* personnel, on the theory that the emphasis was now on costs rather than sales. The real reason was that the salesmen were out in the field and thus could not protect their jobs the way the bureaucrats in the main office could.

In both instances, the needs of the bureaucracy were different from the needs of the firm, and in both instances it was the bureaucracy's needs that were served.

IT COULD BE MAINTAINED that examples drawn from the publishing industry are atypical, since they involve purely governmental producers on the one extreme and on the other, a business which, above almost any other in the "private sector" of the economy, most nearly conforms to the old-fashioned stereotype of owner or entrepreneur management. But, as Corinne Gilb has pointed out in a perceptive book called *Hidden Hierarchies*, the tendency in most large modern industries is for the bureaucracies of industry and government to overlap and then to mesh and ultimately to become indistinguishable. If that is true, and if what I have been arguing is sound, one would expect bureaucratic deflection to be most pronounced in those areas where the private and the public come together. In that expectation, one would not be disappointed.

Let us first consider bureaucratized government and bureaucratized business as antagonists. In 1970 Congress passed the Environmental Protection Act, requiring among other things the establishment and enforcement of minimum standards of safety in the emission of exhaust fumes from automobiles. As a matter of fact no one had more than the smoggiest notion of what safe emission standards were—only one scientific study had been made, and its author was at pains to point out that he was merely offering some educated guesses—but Congress, the very epitome of institutionalized incompetence, passed the law anyway, and required that the standards be met by 1975 and 1976.

Enforcement of the law was entrusted to the Environmental Protection Administration, to the directorship of which President Nixon appointed Mr. William Ruckelshaus. One might have supposed that the EPA, being a brand-new agency and having work to do, would not have suffered from bureaucratic incompetency at the outset; but its very first decision ensured that the law would be unenforceable. The auto makers, faced with some tough standards, suggested that new power plants might be explored—the turbine engine and the Wankel, for example—but the EPA insisted that the conventional internal-combustion engine be continued and cleaned up, lest fooling around with other types of engines be used as an excuse to postpone compliance with the law. As it turned out, compliance would have been relatively easy with other engines but was practically impossible within the confines of the internal-combustion engine: the act required a 90 percent reduction in the emission of hydrocarbons, carbon monoxide, and oxides of nitrogen, but the changes necessary to reduce the first two are quite the reverse of what it takes to reduce the third. It was rather as if economists were required to figure out a way, without interfering with the market or currency systems, of simultaneously doubling wages and lowering prices.

The automotive Big Three—GM, Ford, and Chrysler—for their part, needed little nudging to induce them to stick with the tried and true. From top to bottom, those firms contain enough engineering talent to solve almost any technical problem that mankind is capable of posing; and their managerial talent at the top level is as skilled as any that has ever been assembled. But somehow the managerial and the engineering talents cannot get together when innovation is concerned. Thus even had Ruckelshaus stayed at home, the automotive Big Three would have been stuck with a steadily worsening Same Old Thing.

For the clue to this state of affairs, we must look inside management. The big auto makers, over the years, have striven scrupulously to avoid the bureaucratic artery hardening that has plagued lesser corporations, and have applied both the stick and the carrot toward that end. On the one hand, they have ruthlessly fired managerial personnel who were not doing their jobs; on the other, they have provided abundant incentives for those who performed well. The incentives have increasingly taken the form of tax-free fringe benefits, which amounted by early 1973 to roughly 33 percent of salaries. Verily, personnel on the middle-management level could afford neither to slip nor to go elsewhere; and so General Motors had more talent at that level than did any other large corporation, and Ford and Chrysler were not far behind.

But this is to be noticed, and upper-level management has gradually come to notice it: middle-management personnel is careful to do its job well, but it is equally careful about not taking chances, about not committing itself to anything new, unusual, or experimental. A couple of institutional characteristics of the automotive industry strongly reinforce this conservatism. One is that engine-manufacturing plants are extremely expensive but (unlike stamping plants, used in making auto bodies) are also extremely slow to wear out. Accordingly, engine plants are regarded as permanent capital investment, whereas stamping equipment is treated as an operating cost and amortized in a short period, usually three years. Accordingly, too, the auto makers are as loath to change engine designs as they are eager to change body styles.

The other institutional characteristic of the industry is that the profit margin in automobile manufacturing is exceedingly slim—ranging in the bonanza year 1973 to 2.2 percent of sales at Chrysler to 6.7 percent at General Motors, for a total profit of $3.6 billion on a volume of business well over $70 billion. The extra profit to be made if a particular innovation proves marketable is small, but the loss involved if it is not marketable can transform profits into staggering losses; and it is middle management that bears the brunt of the blame when things go the wrong way. Thus, if top management suggests something radical, middle management is likely to retard its implementation; if a young engineer proposes something radical, middle management is likely to stifle it. And thus the automotive industry, with the best engineering and managerial talent in the world, is stuck on dead center.

The immediate implications of all this are these: the emission standards imposed by the 1970 act, themselves of questionable value, could be met with the internal-combustion engine only by reducing fuel efficiency to nearly zero, and virtually every engineer knew it; and yet the superb talent of the automotive industry and the incompetents in the EPA were equally driven to try to meet the standards through the medium of the internal-combustion engine.

So much for what happens when government and business are antagonists. When they are partners—as they are in defense procurement—things are even worse. Of all the humbugs of our time, fear of the military-industrial complex is the greatest. To be afraid of it is comparable to fearing Louis XVI and Nicholas II; apart from the press, the classroom, and the halls of Congress, there is probably nothing in America to match the Pentagon for incompetence, unless it be the industrialists who supply the Pentagon with weapons that do not work. After four years, for example, the Navy is still waiting for the fifty super-submarines that were to have been built by the Electric Boat Company—which has had trouble with cost overruns already and had yet, at the end of 1973, to lay a single keel. The Army (having virtually abandoned training fighting men in favor of relying on sophisticated weaponry) is still waiting for the supertanks that were to have been built by West Germans and the Chrysler Corporation; apparently the manufacturers are unable to build the tanks with the air conditioning and padded sofas that the Army promised in its recruiting posters. And so on: today's standards are so bad as to make one yearn for the good old days of presunk Victory Ships. At least those ships were occasionally seaworthy, and Kaiser netted only about $100,000 apiece from them.

The Pentagon's relation with the Grumman Corporation is a typical example of the impotence of the military-industrial complex. In the early 1960s Grumman, along with General Dynamics, was awarded a contract for building the swept-wing F-111, which was heralded as the high-performance fighter plane of the 1970s. The man in charge of designing the plane, Grumman engineer Duane Yorke, warned his superiors that it "wasn't going to measure up in virtually every dimension you want to look at, in range performance, in over-all desirability, and in cost." Boeing, he said, had a much better design.

But Grumman's sales department was not interested in making quality airplanes; its specialty was sales, and sell it did. The company's sellers told the Pentagon what the Pentagon wanted to hear, and the Pentagon made the deal. And so, the government bought a plane that was unusable as a fighter and could be used at all only as a not especially effective tactical bomber. Indeed, it got 550 of them, at a cost of $10 billion.

Late in the 1960s the Navy decided it wanted a new fighter plane to replace its highly successful F-4 Phantom. Grumman charged in with a design for the F-14, which was billed as an improved and therefore workable version of the F-111. In fact the F-14 was Grumman Design Number 303, whereas the F-111 was Grumman Design Number 310—which is to say that the F-14 was an *earlier*, not a later, version of the ineffective F-111. And yet the contract for the F-14 was approved as the last weapons system contract awarded by the Johnson administration. The contract price for the F-14, by the way, is $16.8 million per plane—approximately that of the F-111 and more than four times that of the F-4 it replaces.

The saddest thing about these fiascoes is that nobody is especially swindling anybody. If some operator were raking off a billion or two from such deals, we could at least find comfort in the knowledge that a spark of the old-fashioned American spirit remained aglow. Alas, it is not so: the enormous outlay for such enormous bungling is absorbed by workers who would otherwise be idle and by mindless, faceless, nameless bureaucrats—and the great military suppliers are having a hard time making ends meet, even as do you and I.

THE POINT OF ALL THIS is that bureaucratization has satisfied some important social needs but, like the larger no-fail system of which it is a part, locks the nation into irrational and self-destructive economic policies. The ineptness of the military-industrial complex epitomizes the problem: the Pentagon and its suppliers are hopelessly incompetent, and yet institutionally and economically we cannot either allow them to collapse or make them competent. Of course bureaucratization is by no means the sole culprit: other powerful forces have coalesced to supplement bureaucracy in making it institutionally impossible to return to the profit system—or, more properly, to a system based upon requiring each portion of society to earn its own way. The strong and the weak, the competent and the incompetent, the wise and the foolish must all sink or stay afloat together.

Chapter VIII

The Establishment: Who Fleeces Whom?

DURING THE FRENCH GENERAL STRIKE OF 1969, many observers were surprised that it was the Communists who broke the ranks first and thereby, in conjunction with President de Gaulle's tanks, broke the strike. Not so a radical young colleague of mine. "It figures that the Communists would break it," he said; "they're a good establishment party."

I mention the episode by way of introducing organized labor, the welfare system, and the federal tax system as a single subject. What the three phenomena have in common are that each was once a radical innovation, offered by its advocates as an enlightened, humane reform, and that each has become part of the established order, posing a virtually insurmountable barrier to reform, humane or otherwise. Moreover, each constitutes a part of a gigantic institutional trap which is closing in on the American

178

economy and making rational action impossible. Among the symptoms of that trap are absurdities—such as the fact that it has become more economical for the state of Wisconsin to manufacture books at a loss than not to manufacture books at a loss. Now we are about to see how it is cheaper for the Ford Motor Company to pay assembly-line workers $7.50 an hour than it is to pay them $5 an hour, and economical for General Motors to do the same thing and simultaneously pay other workers $5 an hour not to work at all. We shall also see that it would cost more to stop giving away money on welfare programs than to continue giving it away, and that raising and lowering taxes have essentially the same effect on the economy.

LET US BEGIN with organized labor. Not so very long ago, any skeptical treatise on labor unions would have been addressed toward featherbedding and the work ethos on the one hand, and toward the economic and political power of the unions' bosses on the other. Any such criticism, whether once valid or not, is now obsolete. Talk of featherbedding (for example, paying railroad workers a day's wage for each 100 miles traveled, or paying one newspaper typesetter to set the type that is used and another to set type that is promptly discarded) and talk of discouraging productive work (for example, union rules that prohibit proficient bricklayers from laying more bricks in a day than the least proficient can lay) is practically quaint in these Enlightened Times. After all, the entire city of Detroit—the nation in microcosm—is a featherbed, for the work done by the 800,000 people in the automobile industry could be done as well, and probably better, by machines and a work force of perhaps 150,000. To make such a change, of course, would be so disruptive as to be unthinkable, and the United Auto Workers would not let it happen.

As to the unions' power, the economic has been curtailed both by legislative enactment and by the processes of industrial evolution, and the political was always overrated. Organized labor's economic power had already crested by the time of the passage of the Taft-Hartley Act in 1947; its power to deliver votes may have helped elect Harry Truman in 1948, but it was unable to defeat Senator Robert Taft in 1950, unable to bring Michigan to support Adlai Stevenson in 1952 or 1956, and unable to swing a single state in the presidential election of 1972.

But somewhere along the way the unions became a part of the establishment. For one thing, the technostructure of the more mature industries came to recognize that the presence of a strong union made the management of workers a great deal easier. Unionization made it possible for workers to retain a sense of independence, individuality, "otherness"; but also made it possible for management to deal with workers efficiently and impersonally, as if they were machines. This was brought home to me forcibly in the mid-sixties, when I heard the labor vice-president of a major steel company describe what a joy it was to deal with David McDonald, president of the United Steel Workers union, as opposed to the chaotic labor relations that had prevailed before unionization and still prevailed in the few plants in which workers were unionized by crafts. For a second thing, executives of labor unions have come to be accorded influence in the political process that befits their status, rather than their capacity to deliver; and thus administrators and congressmen pay appropriate deference to Leonard Woodcock of the UAW even as they do to Richard Gerstenberg, chairman of General Motors, though in a campaign Woodcock can no more deliver votes than Gerstenberg can deliver money.

It would be a mistake, however, to regard organized labor as no longer a vital part of the economy simply because it has become an essentially passive part. In at least five important ways, unionization has fundamentally and permanently altered the structure and operation of modern American corporate business enterprise.

First, unionization has altered the cost structure of manufacturing. Before unionization, fixed costs in a manufacturing enterprise (taxes and costs of servicing capital investment, such as interest and depreciation) were relatively trivial; what was important were variable costs, those that increased or decreased with the volume of production, principally labor and raw materials. Nowadays, what with the guaranteed annual wage that the automotive industry and the UAW pioneered in the late 1950s, together with escalator clauses, seniority rules, employers' contributions to unemployment insurance, and the like, labor has become much more nearly a fixed cost. To illustrate the change, let us suppose that widget makers were once employed by the American Widget Company at $50 a week, or $2500 a year, and that the average worker could turn out 1000 widgets a year—or a unit labor cost of $2.50 per widget. Suppose the widget market fluctuated between zero and 100,000; if there was no market for widgets at all, the manufacturer employed no workers at all, and if there was a market for 100,000 widgets he employed 100 workers. Most of the time, of course, the market would have been somewhere between the extremes, and the employer hired or fired, and thus raised or lowered his labor cost, accordingly. The selling price of the widget would be set at a level that would yield the manufacturer essentially the same profit per unit, no matter how many widgets were sold.

To oversimplify for the moment, unionization has so changed things that the widget manufacturer now has to pay his workers 40 to 60 percent of a year's wages whether they make any widgets or not. To the extent that workers have to be paid irrespective of their output, wages become a fixed rather than a variable cost.

The effects of that development are accentuated by another aspect of modern business, one that is not directly related to labor. Since the late 1930s, as a means of enlarging the demand for their products, manufacturers of consumer durables have resorted increasingly to "built-in obsolescence," mainly in the form of changes in styles and fashions. The practice and the effects of it can be seen in everything from electric toasters to clothing, but can most clearly be illustrated in the automobile industry, where "model changeovers" take place roughly every three years, and minor stylistic changes are made every year. The cost of retooling for such changes is enormous, running into the hundreds of millions, but since the investment is short-lived it must be treated as an operating cost, not a permanent capital investment, and must therefore be recovered out of sales. That creates another major fixed cost, one that does not vary with the volume of production. The only important remaining variable cost, raw materials, is a relatively small portion of the total cost. As a result, automobile manufacturers have to sell a very large number of cars to break even—that is, to meet their fixed costs—but after they exceed what is called the get-out point something like three quarters of every dollar of gross sales is net profit.

A second change resulting from the maturation of unionization is likewise related to other forces, being partly a function of the first, partly a function of unionization itself, and partly a function of government policy. I refer to fringe benefits, as they are called, to such things as the employers' contributions to medical insurance, life insurance, Social Security, and so on. At General Motors these range from 28 to 33 percent of wages and salaries—which means that to pay a worker $5 an hour costs the company about $6.50 an hour. But that is not all: there are other costs as well. The employer is required to pay Social Security taxes on each employee, and also to keep and report a wide variety of records on each, with the average result that it takes one new filing clerk or paper-shuffler to service ten new employees. Each filing clerk, of course, has his own fringe benefits, and every ten filing clerks necessitate an eleventh.

For these reasons, increased production does not often create new jobs, at least in big established industries. When, late in 1971, President Nixon announced Phase I of his New Economic Policy—freezing prices and wages, floating the dollar, devaluing by 10 percent, and so on— the prime beneficiaries were expected to be the automobile makers and their suppliers, and a lot of statistics were tossed around to prove that every *x* additional automobiles sold would yield *y* new jobs. Automobile production increased even more than expected, but employment in the industry remained essentially constant. What happened was this: the Big Three automotive manufacturers found it was cheaper to pay their existing workers to work overtime at time and a half (which is to say, at half again their usual hourly wages) than to take on the costs of increasing plant capacity and servicing the extra fringe benefits, the extra obligations, the training, and the additional bookkeeping that would have been involved in hiring new employees.*

And yet, for similar reasons, cutting production can reduce employment. In the early winter of 1973–74, for example, when the implications of the fuel crisis began to register with consumers, demand for big cars plummeted and demand for smaller cars rose apace. General Motors curtailed production of Oldsmobiles and Cadillacs and laid off tens of thousands of workers in its big-car plants, even though its union contract required the company to pay the idled workers 95 percent of their weekly wages— for that was more economical than paying the workers to make products that could not be sold. Meanwhile, GM continued to pay workers overtime wages in small-car

---

* By emphasizing the labor factor in this phenomenon I do not mean to belittle the importance of the cost of increasing plant capacity. The industry is "engine-bound," which is to say that its engine-manufacturing capacity is limited and much of it is not designed for twenty-four-hour operations. Operating two eleven-hour shifts, interrupted by an hour apiece for clearing waste and bringing in new materials, is often the most efficient arrangement.

184

plants. Moreover, that situation was not likely to pass quickly, for the workers could not be reabsorbed until plant capacity for smaller cars was increased—and it takes three years to build a new plant.

The third change is implicit in the first two: wage increases are immediately inflationary only to the extent that they increase aggregate buying power, and only gradually as a part of a cost structure that can be passed on to consumers. That is to say, at any given time the makers of a particular product will be charging all the traffic will bear—or, more accurately, the highest price they can get consistent with optimum sales. Thus when wage increases push up their costs of production, prices cannot be raised commensurately. Accordingly, the increased cost must be absorbed by decreasing profits, at least until the rising level of wages in the economy as a whole makes consumers willing to pay more. To management that is less concerned with profits than with expansion for its own sake, this is nothing to fret about. Only in the over-all view—which it is to *nobody's* immediate interest to take—is the matter worth worrying about.

The fourth result of unionization has been the creation of a caste system which locks people in, and locks people out, of functions and careers and rank and status, almost as decisively as people were locked in or out during the Middle Ages—thus exacerbating the tendency, begun during the New Deal, to freeze Americans into their existing relative positions. Labor unions in the United States are organized upon two quite opposite principles, the craft principle and the industry principle. In the first, all the workers in a given locale who have a particular skill—

185

such as carpentering or operating linotype machines—belong to a single union, even though their employers may be many different persons or firms. In the second, all persons who work in a particular industry—ranging from diggers to crane operators to time-card punchers in a coal mine—belong to a single union, regardless of their special function. Until the late 1930s, industrial unions were regarded as the poor relations of the craft unions; thereafter, until the late 1950s, the two regarded one another as natural rivals; and since then the AFL has merged with the CIO, with about as much mutual trust as one might expect from a Pan-Semitic Union of Arabs and Jews.

The craft unions, the AFL part of the AFL-CIO, are extremely exclusive. Carpentry, for example, is not so simple as merely hitting a nail on the head with a hammer, but long ago the carpenters' union closed ranks and made a full-fledged mystery of the craft, and by virtue of their bargaining power the carpenters have been able to dictate who is, and who is not, to be regarded as a bona fide carpenter. That power to dictate forced the wages of carpenters (along with those of electricians, plumbers, stereotypers, and bricklayers) up to $10 and $15 an hour, and also froze out of the union all aspiring craftsmen who did not have the proper qualifications by birth or marriage. Outsiders—such members of the urban labor force, for example, as blacks and Puerto Ricans—simply do not get in, despite the Civil Rights Act of 1964.

The industrial unions, to be sure, are more democratic —unless one happens, as most American city dwellers do, to be black or Puerto Rican, or to be Appalachian white, or otherwise to be relatively new upon the scene in the

northern industrial areas. What works against the new-comer is the seniority principle. In the old days, before the union, employers were apt to fire workers for their loyalty to the union principle, no matter how long and hard they had worked; and so, when industrial unions came to be recognized, workers understandably demanded that employment tenure be based upon length of service, irrespective of the political or union sympathies of the employees. In due course, this demand was incorporated into contracts, with a provision that after employees work a specified number of consecutive days—ninety-one in the UAW, for example—they acquire "seniority" and job pro-tection.

Gradually it dawned upon assembly-line workers that the seniority principle could be used the other way around, to keep people out as well as protect those who were in. If it were so used, industrial workers would be in the same position as their elite brothers in the craft unions: they could control their membership. Now, what I am about to say is consistently denied by officials of the UAW, but it is a fact that black and Appalachian white workers are regularly denied the opportunity to work for the ninety-one days required under UAW contracts, and the same practice is common in every other industrial-type union that I know about except the Teamsters.

As a consequence, several million people, mostly of minority races and ethnic groups, have a status that is subproletarian. That is to say, they are not even at the bottom of the ladder in the modern industrial system—they are *outside* the system. Moreover, they appear to be perma-nently locked out, for there is no way to take them into

the system without undermining the institutionalized security of those on the inside.

Which brings us to the fifth major union-related development. Until the middle 1960s, it appeared that those workers outside the union system had some hope, for the expansion of jobs that lent themselves to blue-collar unionization had passed its peak: the future seemed to reside in the more flexible area of nonunion employment. Though practically all industrial workers were unionized by 1954, only 35.1 percent of the country's nonagricultural workers belonged to unions, and in the next decade the percentage steadily declined. But then the union movement got a new lease on life in the form of public employees.

At first it was easy to belittle efforts to unionize public employees, for they lacked the crucial coercive weaponry that other workers had. My father, who spent most of his adult life as a dedicated dispatcher in the postal service, was fond of misquoting Calvin Coolidge to the effect that "there is no right, by anyone, anytime, anywhere, to strike against public service or the public safety." More to the point, to strike against government seemed inherently futile, since the power to appropriate money rests in city councils, state legislatures, and the Congress, which represent the sovereign people and not the school boards or bureaucrats who are the public employees' "management." The illusion vanished in the late sixties, when policemen and firemen forced the acceptance of their demands by developing epidemics of "blue flu," and schoolteachers, garbage collectors, post office employees, and transit workers demonstrated their power to immobilize vast segments

of society. Since then, unionization of public employees has grown astronomically, and the number of jobs available to "outsiders" has shrunk in proportion thereto. One more door is being closed.

To be sure, several areas of unionized public employment are dominated by blacks. But the critical point is that even in those areas, an ever growing portion of the population is being frozen into position, even as large numbers are frozen outside the system.

WHAT WE DO when we encounter a problem in America is attack it directly and avoid looking for (or at) any underlying malaise—which is to say, perhaps, that reform follows the lines of least resistance. Hence, when it began to be suspected, during Eisenhower's presidency or Kennedy's, that goodly numbers of Americans were outside the system, we repeatedly "passed a law" (another American habit) declaring them inside the system, but otherwise could think of nothing more imaginative than to offer them money as compensation for the oversight. That degrading bribe—to remain outside and shut up—was advanced not merely toward the institutionally frozen-out able-bodied adult males, but toward most other outsiders as well. Young people were bribed to go to college, old people to retire, unwed mothers to stay off the job market and breed some more.

Thus was born what is sometimes called the welfare mess. It has been widely publicized that in our proudest city, New York, more than one person in five collects welfare payments of one sort or another; less publicized is the fact that by 1971 welfare expenditures constituted nearly that proportion of the entire economy. In that year, the combined federal and state governmental expenditure for social welfare was in excess of $170 billion, out of a gross national product of just over a trillion dollars and a gross national income of $850 billion. In other words, nearly one American dollar in five was used to pay people to do nothing at all—not merely to do something useless, such as sorting papers for people who themselves do nothing except sort papers, but to do *nothing at all,* and not aspire to rock the boat by doing something.

I do not propose to pass moral judgment upon this scheme of things; I am concerned here not with morality but with economics. A learned and esteemed friend of mine, when confronted with the statement, "Well, a person has to stay alive," habitually responds, "Why?" I shan't be so cruel, but I would point out that only three things happen when anybody gives anybody else something for nothing. The first is that the giver feels mightily virtuous. The second and third are that the recipients (a) hate the donor and (b) come to expect the donations as a matter of right. Accordingly, the welfare mothers of Michigan organized a union two years ago to go on "strike" and angrily demanded "raises," and the governor of the state apologetically negotiated with the ladies and urged the legislature to listen to their demands.

But all that lies in the area of noneconomic aspects of the welfare system, and is economically unimportant. What is economically important is that we are stuck with the system. Theoretically we might resort to an older ethic and let all who cannot support themselves die, except that the cost would be prohibitive, what with the legalized ex-

penses of burial and what with the benefits legally accruing to survivors. More seriously, if we scrapped the entire
welfare system the consequences would be as disruptive as,
say, shutting down the automotive industry. One direct
result would be to increase unemployment by several hundred thousand, for that many people are employed full
time in superintending the disbursal of welfare payments.
Another result would be to reduce aggregate personal
buying power by a staggering 11.5 percent—producing
roughly the same effect as if personal income taxes were
doubled and the federal government sat on the proceeds.
In other words, we cannot afford it.

The conservative economist Milton Friedman has proposed a negative income tax as a means of reforming the
system, and President Nixon himself asked Congress to
pass a variation of Friedman's proposal, in the form of a
minimum annual wage. All such proposals would give
everybody (or at least the poor) some minimal sum, say
$3000 per year per family, and allow them to keep half
of what they earned up to some other figure, say $6000.
Soon or late, everyone who proposes such a scheme figures
out the arithmetic involved, and notices that people would
learn that it would be less profitable to work than not to
work; and so the innovators retreat behind blushing faces
and quietly withdraw their proposals. It could, to be sure,
be turned around. Everybody (or the poor) could be given
$3000 a year, and be paid a dollar for every dollar they
earn above that, up to a certain sum, and so be provided
with powerful incentive to work. But that would just
make things worse, for the fundamental problem is that

we have too little work to be done and too many workers to do it.

The welfare system is therefore here to stay—in one form or another. Recipients of money for nothing, of course, have little bargaining power apart from their votes, and so tend to fall behind as the spiral of inflation moves inexorably upward. Accordingly, Congress and the state legislatures periodically compensate the old folks and the unemployed and the unwed mothers by raising their "fixed" incomes by 15 or 20 percent. Indeed, since 1971, "transfer payments," as economists euphemistically call taking money from people who do work and using it to pay people not to work, have been rising half again as fast as wages and salaries. The ensuing increase in aggregate buying power, in turn, adds to the inflationary pressures already created by wheeler-dealers, defense suppliers, bureaucrats, unions, and all the rest, and in time makes welfare recipients ever more dependent upon an ever increasing dole.

AND NOW, TAXES—a subject on which there are even more theories than theorists. A few general propositions can readily be agreed upon. Taxes tend to go up rather than down. Most people figure they are desirable when other people have to pay them. Most people will pay them if avoiding them is too dangerous or more expensive than paying them. Liberal economists incline to believe the more the merrier, conservative economists the less the better. Progressive taxation is either good or bad, depending upon one's predisposition: generally speaking, the higher one's income rises, the less appealing progressive taxation becomes. The federal income tax, being progressive, punishes people for being rich; the Social Security tax, being regressive, punishes people for being poor. And so on.

More soberly and substantively, in the mainstream of modern Western economic theory there are two, and only two, serious schools of thought regarding taxation. The first is that represented by Colin Clark in his *Limits of Taxable Capacity* and, more recently and more entertainingly, by C. Northcote Parkinson in his *Law and the Profits*. The gist of this argument is that there is a theoretical point (Clark sets it at 25 to 27 percent of national income) at which taxation becomes counterproductive, stimulates inflation more than it increases government revenues, destroys incentive, encourages tax evasion, undermines respect for government, and even incites the taxpayers to revolt or revolution.

Taxes in the United States, having reached 19.3 percent of national income (17 percent of gross national product) in 1939, climbed to 23.8 percent of national income in 1949, rose steadily until they reached 35.5 percent in 1969, and are projected at 36.5 percent in 1974. It can be argued—and perhaps demonstrated—that they have produced all the deleterious effects that were predicted, short of revolution; but I submit that they have done their worst, at least for the time being. That is to say, the effects of every future increase, within broad limits, will be progressively less dramatic.

The opposite school of thought, that broadly describable as Keynesian, has had far more adherents and is far more important. The Keynesians either denied the effects predicted by the likes of Clark and Parkinson or dismissed the effects as essentially unimportant. The Keynesian model runs something like this. After taxes are raised to a sufficient level (say 15 or 20 percent of national income), they can be manipulated to produce every manner of desired effect. When the economy is sluggish, economic growth can be stimulated and employment expanded by lowering taxes, either in the form of a cut in personal income taxes (which increases consumer buying power) or in the form of reduced corporate taxes (which stimulates increased investment). When the economy becomes overheated—which is to say, when pressures of cost and demand become potent enough to be inflationary—taxes can be raised, which has a cooling and deflationary effect. In practice, it turned out that there was constant tension between inflation and unemployment—that there was always one or the other—but the theorists worked out formulas for "acceptable" inflation and "tolerable" unemployment, and proceeded to use the magical instrument of tax manipulation to steer a happy middle course. The philosopher's stone appeared to have been found at last: a means of ending the devastating business cycle, which had long been regarded as an evil but necessary concomitant of the otherwise perfect capitalistic system, and substituting for it economic growth at a controlled rate and with "full" employment and "acceptable" inflation.

It is true that a couple of bugs infested the system. One was that Republicans and Democrats, though both ultimately embraced Keynesianism, differed rather sharply in their notions of what was acceptable inflation and tolerable unemployment. That is, Republicans tended toward the view that virtually no inflation was acceptable and that a great deal of unemployment was tolerable; Democrats tended just the other way. Another bug was what some economists call the "it won't be done" argument: that politicians will not cool the economy by raising taxes when necessary, which has been the case in practice. In 1964, for example, President Johnson made the commitment to Keynesianism official by pushing through Congress a large tax cut, which had the desired effect of stimulating an economy that had become sluggish. It is to be noted that 1964 was an election year, and tax cuts are normally popular with the voters. Two years later, however, the economy was rapidly becoming overheated, for (in part because of the Vietnamese War) inflation was getting out of hand. Keynesian principles now dictated an increase in taxes, but 1966 too was an election year, and the tax increase was not forthcoming. Quite properly, in the realm of theory, Keynesians insist that the "it won't be done" argument does not impair the validity of the model. In truth, the flaw could be remedied by depoliticizing the federal income tax in the same way the tariff was depoliticized sixty years ago—namely, by placing the matter under the control of a commission rather than of Congress.

But the bugs in the system, alas, are not its principal weakness. The principal weakness is that, like pragmatism, it does not work. For two or three years now economists have been fretting over the fact that inflation and unemployment (which the Keynesian model posits as antithetical) have learned to walk hand in hand. The reasons are not at all difficult to discover; all one has to do is forget about an abstraction called the "economy" and look at the economics of running any particular business enterprise. The effects of President Nixon's Phase I economic policy upon the automotive industry is a case in point.

What is even more telling, the manipulation of taxes (or, for that matter, of the money supply) has lost most of its power either to reduce prices or to increase investment and employment. The inability to drive prices down is readily explicable: the upward pressures in the economy are simply too powerful to be curtailed, short of a tax level that is entirely confiscatory. If personal taxes were raised 10 or even 20 percent, consumer cash buying power would be reduced, but that would not lower the costs of producing and distributing goods. Many consumers would use their credit to buy now against next year's inflation and anticipated raises, and at least some of the increased tax revenues would find their way back into the economy. The remaining slack would have to be absorbed out of business profits—and most corporations would try to overcome their losses by increasing prices.

The reasons for the decreased ability to stimulate the economy are less obvious. The essence of the problem lies in the internal economics of large corporate industrial firms, and most particularly in the interrelated facts that such firms (a) have large gross revenues in relation to capital investment, and yet (b) have progressively moved toward higher fixed costs in relation to variable costs. As a result of the first, the principal tax device for stimulating investment—fast write-off of capital expenditures—has become of relatively small consequence save in the few kinds of businesses which remain capital-intensive, notably utilities and, to a lesser extent, the metals industries. As a result of the second, manufacturers take their profits mainly at the tail end of the run—that is, after 20,000 books or 50,000 television sets or 100,000 automobiles of a particular style have been sold. Thus when disposable personal income is increased by a cut in personal income taxes, the public buys the 25,000th book, the 60,000th television set, the 120,000th automobile; but no new jobs are created, nor do prices rise or fall. All that happens is that corporate profits increase.

To be sure, the slow, steady, inexorable rise in the tax level has both pushed and pulled the over-all price level slowly, steadily, and inexorably upward. But, what is more important for our immediate purposes, the manipulation of taxes within reasonable limits has lost the power to effect a corresponding increase or decrease in either employment or prices.

In simpler times, when the tax level was below 15 or perhaps even 10 percent of national income, manipulation of taxes had little effect and manipulation of interest rates was potentially an effective device for controlling economic growth, employment, and prices. Beyond that tax level, manipulation of interest rates proved largely futile (except for inducing recessions), and manipulation of taxes was efficacious. Beyond some other level, probably in the range of 35 percent, manipulation of taxes became equally futile—not so much because of taxation itself, but because an economy that has become so large and so institutionalized that it can support taxes at that level has become too large and too institutionalized to control with minor tax changes.

The efficacy of taxation in causing economic change is

thus, for practical purposes, reduced to selective change through the so-called substitution effect. Simply put, government can (at least theoretically) cause people to buy or produce one thing rather than another by raising or lowering taxes on specific items. Some historians hold that Americans drink coffee rather than tea because of Parliament's tea tax of 1773; probably they could be induced to shift back to tea if Congress were to levy a tax on coffee of $5 a pound. Similarly, if the market for widgets and gismos is equal, manufacturers can be driven to produce widgets and not gismos by making the tax on the profits of producing one zero and the other 100 percent. More tangibly, Congress could solve quite a number of problems and effect some fundamental social as well as economic changes by imposing a tax of a dollar a gallon on gasoline.

The most conspicuous, complex, and important example of the use of this power concerns the petroleum industry, or more properly the business of discovering and producing crude oil and natural gas. All mining, including that of oil and natural gas, is different from other business activity in one crucial respect: what miners have to sell is their irreplaceable capital. Quite prudently, the federal government does not ordinarily tax capital, on the theory that to do so would be to destroy future sources of revenue (the only significant exceptions being "capital gains" taxes and inheritance taxes). And yet, not to tax the proceeds from the sale of mine output seems illogical, since the proceeds are in fact income and since the capital is progressively dried up in any event. Once a mine or an oil

field is exhausted, it produces no more revenue for anyone.

The oil and gas business has another peculiarity that is
not common even among other mining enterprises. By
and large, we know where the coal, gold, diamonds, iron,
and bauxite of the world are located; we do not know
where the oil and gas are, though seismographic and other
surveys have shown us the places where they can be. The
chances of finding oil, even in one of the places it can be,
are one in ten. Drilling for oil, a dry hole or a wet one,
costs a lot of money, and the costs increase with the depths,
which in modern times are deep indeed. Now, the question arises whether, for tax purposes, drilling costs are to
be regarded as capital investment or operating expense. If
they are the latter they should properly be deductible
against income; but in either event, how should the costs
of drilling nine dry holes be reckoned as against the enormous profits that ensue from the one wet hole?

In sum, keeping the books on the business involves
some complex problems in accounting theory and in the
theory of tax liability: none of the rules seems to fit. As it
happened, when Congress designed the laws governing
taxation of the oil business, it decided to ignore questions
of equitable accounting and to concentrate on a matter of
larger national concern, namely, the encouragement of
exploration and discovery of the oil and gas resources
which are so vital to the functioning of the entire economy.
Toward that end, a number of gimmicks were built into
the tax system. As the law currently stands, the most important of these gimmicks are three. (1) The investor is
allowed to treat as operating expense almost the full cost

of drilling the well—the so-called intangible drilling expenses, essentially everything but the cost of leasing the land—and thus to deduct against current income what is in effect the purchase price of a valuable asset. (2) When oil or gas is produced from the well, 22 percent of the net income is exempt from taxes as an allowance for depletion of the capital investment. (3) If the investor sells his rights to the producing well, half of his profit is exempt from all taxes and the other half is treated as a long-term capital gain, taxable at a mere 25 percent.

Several peculiarities about this scheme of things want notice. In the first place, by virtue of it, the one industry on which the nation is most totally dependent is almost wholly politicized. The survival of the industry hinges entirely upon profitability, and profitability hinges, in turn, almost entirely on the tax laws. Not upon rational planning, or upon skill, perseverance, talent, training, knowledge, good management, or even luck. Just the tax laws.

The tax laws, in their turn, hinge upon politics, and in no small measure politics hinges upon money. As it happens, corporate money is politically sterile—under the various corrupt-practices acts, corporations are effectively prohibited from making political contributions—but individual money is highly fertile, and the oil and gas industry is the one business in which the flow of money is primarily personal rather than corporate. To be sure, in 1972 the Republican National Committee, through Maurice Stans and Herbert Kalmbach, was able to pry millions in illegal contributions from various corporations—including $40,-000 from Goodyear, $100,000 from Gulf, $55,000 from American Airlines, $40,000 from Braniff, $30,000 from

Minnesota Mining & Manufacturing, and so on. But that was extremely unusual; and what is more important, the fact that corporate managers were willing to risk jail sentences out of fear of the Nixon fund-raisers is an indication of their lack of political clout, not political strength. Several of the contributing companies, for example, were under FTC or Justice Department investigations. Independent oil people, by contrast, lay out their contributions on their own terms, and expect suitable favors in return. In other words, oilmen as individuals have a lot of money and they can and do spend a great deal of it to elect representatives who will vote to continue the existing tax arrangements.

One more thing: the system works, or rather it did until recently. Between the end of World War II and 1972, the United States never had more than a ten years' supply of proved sources of gas and oil, and yet the drillers kept coming up with enough to provide for the nation's enormous and ever growing needs.

But they are not finding it any more, for another element has entered the equation: the antibusiness mentality, the tradition of Bolingbroke, Jefferson, Jackson, Bryan, and the second Roosevelt. Increasingly, muckraking pop economists have attacked the oil and gas tax system as a "great treasury raid," as if the industry's profits properly belonged to the people, by which is meant the government. Increasingly, too, those parts of government which are outside the political influence of the industry have begun to whittle away at the shelters in the tax system—as the Tax Court, and then the Federal Circuit Court for the

Second District, and then the Internal Revenue Service did in 1972.

Selective tax manipulation is a powerful weapon, far too powerful to be entrusted to the largely irresponsible processes of politics. Virtually every other aspect of the economy has built-in institutional checks, and though institutional forces have put one part of the economy after another in a straitjacket, at least their pressures are predictable. In the most crucial economic area of all, that of the fossil fuel supply, both the pressures and the resulting policies are entirely unpredictable. The consequences become more visible almost daily. Our largest single source of fossil fuel energy, bituminous coal, was virtually wiped out (at least temporarily) when antipollution laws were passed in response to the pressure of environmentalists. And, as we shall see, the oil crisis of 1973–74—as well as the far more portentious underlying shortage—resulted in large measure from the vagaries of politics.

ADAM SMITH SUGGESTED, in *The Wealth of Nations*, that it was possible for a country to become so rich that its economy would simply cease to function. We are getting there. Our main device for economic regulation does not work, our institutions paralyze us, our noninstitutionalized efforts are subject to arbitrary and capricious destruction. But the worst is yet to come, for we have been invaded by saviors.

Chapter IX

Of Luddites and Barnburners

IF THE AMERICAN PEOPLE had been more aware of their history, and therefore less the victims of it, they might have been prepared for the orgy of self-criticism to which they subjected themselves in the 1960s. Much as we pretend to worship success, we are programmed by our culture to hate the winner and cheer the underdog, and we do so most vigorously whenever the winner is ourselves. In bad times—when we seem to be losing—we usually band together, reavow our faith in our system, and find it easy to discover and oppose our enemies. In good times, we cherish the sentiment that "we have met the enemy and he is us," and warmly embrace those who tell us how wicked we are and promise to save us from ourselves.

Thus it was that in 1961 John F. Kennedy could strike responsive chords by calling upon America to get off its duff and start doing its duty to mankind, after a generation of merely defeating militarily the various tyrants of the world, footing the bill for rebuilding a war-torn planet, and spreading comfort to a high proportion of our own population into the bargain. The "best and the brightest" generation of Americans, hearing the call, proceeded to make rather a botch of its crusade to save the world; but at home it was superlatively successful in convincing Americans that they were a blight in Paradise.

It was in this atmosphere of feeling guilty about winning that the distinguished marine biologist Rachel Carson launched an attack upon the very fundaments of our postindustrial civilization, in a series of articles in *The New Yorker* magazine that were subsequently published as a book called *Silent Spring*. From an economic and scientific point of view, Miss Carson was important in calling attention to the stepchild science of ecology, whose main message is the essentially unscientific one that things are interconnected in myriad and complex ways, and thus that actions have all sorts of consequences beyond the immediate range of cause and effect. For instance, we increase crop yields by spraying with DDT, but the chemical tends to concentrate in insects which are eaten by fish and birds that humans eat, and so our food is unsafe; and yet if we stop using DDT, gypsy moths devour our forests. From a socio-politico-ecological point of view, however, what Miss Carson did was give birth to the environmentalist movement and a related phenomenon that came to be called consumerism, and to the most destructive progeny and protagonist of both movements, Mr. Ralph Nader.

Nader, then about thirty years old, had been hanging

around Washington for some time when *Silent Spring* appeared. As his semiofficial biographer put it, his life had been "very much like that of the sort of agent who is called, in intelligence work, a 'fictitious'—someone who is sent to another country with instructions to build an identity while awaiting orders." He obtained a job as a $50-a-day consultant for Assistant Secretary of Labor Daniel Moynihan, in which capacity he used the notes and articles his boss had produced, added some ideas of his own, and came up with a book on American automobiles, published in 1965 and called *Unsafe at Any Speed.*

In that work Nader attacked the safety of American motor vehicles and demonstrated them to be unsafe, indeed. Of course, "indeed" is a shifty index, of safety or of anything else. Somehow, in his concern for the engineering of American cars, Nader neglected to mention that accident rates, injury rates, and death rates *per passenger mile* are far lower in the United States than in other Western or Westernized nations. Nor, from a strictly scientific point of view, or even from the narrower view of engineering efficiency, did Nader demonstrate that highway fatalities are socially detrimental. For one thing, who can name a single eminent statesman or scholar, scientist or engineer, or businessman or labor leader who was killed or seriously injured in an automobile accident? The vast majority of highway deaths, in fact, are of persons between eighteen and thirty years of age. Now, most thinking people, myself and I suppose Mr. Nader included, regard it as imperative that the worldwide population explosion be checked. The usual prescription toward that end is birth control and liberalized abortion—which is to say, preventing people from being born. Who, however, is to say that that method is statistically more likely to improve the quality of the human race than permitting, nay encouraging, the destruction of persons who happen already to have been born between 1943 and 1956 and are now of prime breeding age? Everybody knows that there were too many people born during those years, anyway.

In any event, no one paid much attention to the book until the early spring of 1966, when it was revealed that General Motors had hired private detectives to pry into Nader's personal life, harass him, and discredit him. Forthwith, his book became a best seller, he became a hero and a martyr, and Congress took up his recommendations. Nader was supported by Senator Abraham Ribicoff of Connecticut, who had established a minor reputation as a champion of highway safety (as governor of his state he had instituted a crackdown that increased the suspension of driver's licenses from 372 to 10,055 in one year, though unfortunately the accident rate went up anyway), and also by Bobby Kennedy and Lyndon Johnson. The result was the Traffic and Motor Vehicle Safety Act of 1966, which required that various safety features be built into all motor vehicles sold in the United States after January 1, 1968.

There was rather more to all this than was reported in newspaper headlines. For one thing, most of the safety devices required by the new law could be readily engineered into cars of American manufacture, at costs that could be passed along to buyers. On the other hand most foreign automobiles, which were capturing a sixth or a seventh of the American market, could not meet the new standards except through fundamental enlargement and redesign, which would destroy their competitive position. In other words, there are some things that you can put on a Chevrolet or a Buick that you cannot put on a Volkswagen or a Toyota. And there was more. Big cars (American or foreign) could meet the standards more easily than could small cars, and the profit margin on the larger was greater; and sales of the optional safety equipment recommended (but at first not required) by the law could increase the profit margin of all American automobiles by 25 to 50 percent. In the first five years after the act became effective, the safety devices cost the consumer approximately $20 billion—not including the additional gasoline burned by ever heavier cars—and the fatal accident rate is still climbing. To paraphrase Voltaire, if Nader had not existed, it would have been profitable for General Motors to have invented him.

Persistent rumors in Detroit held that General Motors had in fact invented Nader, in a modern variation of the ancient Brer Rabbit theme. The payoff, according to this school of skepticism, came with the $26 million suit that Nader brought against the company for its harassment of him; he had not a chance of winning, but General Motors chose to settle out of court by paying him $425,000 in *tax-free* damages. Afterward, he reciprocated by attacking Volkswagen as the unsafest car of all. Be that as it may, the industry profited from the encounter in the short run, and since then Nader has made upward of $200,000 a year from lectures as a champion of the lowly consumer— and has been allowed to avoid paying income taxes on those earnings by establishing himself as a public trust, with himself as the "managing trustee."

A POPULAR STEREOTYPE has the man of principle fighting for a cause until he becomes corrupted by the opportunity for wealth offered by the System. In real life corruption more commonly comes the other way, when a wholesome, 100 percent red-blooded American con man plays the part of the Messiah so long and successfully that he begins to believe he is a Messiah.

In the two or three years after his profitable "confrontation" with General Motors, Ralph Nader crusaded for legislation to protect the consumer against the corporate monsters who dominated a variety of fields. At least six congressional enactments can be attributed directly to his influence—the Wholesome Meat Act, the Wholesome Poultry Act, the Natural Gas Pipeline Act, the Radiation Control for Health and Safety Act, the Occupational Safety and Health Act, and the Coal Mine Health and Safety Act. None of these laws rectified the conditions they were ostensibly designed to improve, all added to the bureaucratic snarl, most profited the industries they were designed to punish, and some proved detrimental to the consumer. The Wholesome Meat Act, for example, effectively vested the several states with power to control the amount of impurities allowed in intrastate meats—unless, as in the case of Michigan, the state government chose to impose standards higher than those required by the federal government for meat sold in interstate commerce. The effect of the act was to force Michigan to lower its standards.

According to his biographer, Nader learned from such experiences that bringing change in a complex modern society requires more than simply passing another law, and so redirected his efforts toward an attack upon the whole American system. Another way to view it is that he opened a franchise operation. Enlisting the aid of reform-minded college students (recruited mainly from law schools), he set loose teams of Nader's Raiders to dig up dirt on a wide range of corporations and government agencies. The Raiders, employing tactics reminiscent of those of the late Senator Joseph R. McCarthy, grabbed headline after headline with sensational charges of corruption and incompetence. Nader calls their technique "Advocacy Scholarship," which as often as not is a euphemism for the Big Lie. On more careful investigation than Nader devoted to the subject, for instance, it turns out that none of the charges he levied against the Corvair—his favorite target in *Unsafe at Any Speed*—was well-founded; and his Raiders were likewise more devoted to advocacy than to scholarship.

Nader's next step, subsidized by grants from a number of tax-free foundations, was to organize the Center for Study of Responsive Law, Public Interest Research Groups (PIRG) in several states, and a variety of related organizations; soon he was running a $2.5 million annual operation. Inspired by his example, other reformers all over the nation formed similar groups—aimed at protecting consumers, forcing corporations to be more responsive to the demands of customers and stockholders, and protecting the environment against pollution and the rape of Mother Nature.

Faced with such unanticipated demands for change, the establishment (that is, organized society) responded with the technique that Herbert Marcuse has described as co-option. To co-opt is to take over the language of opposition and turn it to the use of the system being opposed. When Shell Oil Company sponsors TV advertisements suggesting that its main function as a corporation is cleaning up oil spills and protecting wildlife, the effort to co-opt is clumsy and readily spotted. When elected officials adopt the language of protest to describe what they are doing, most of us buy it.

The co-opted movement caught on with astonishing quickness. When Nader first began to attract attention to himself and his causes, he ran at best a poor third behind civil rights and Vietnam. But then, in the late sixties, the Hertz and the Avis of the cause business ran out of gas, which is to say that the racial question exploded and the war question fizzled. Simultaneously, Nixon and virtually every congressman pledged themselves to the cause (they were treated as one) of consumerism and environmentalism. The turning point came in May of 1970, with the "massacres" at Kent State and Jackson State: the feebleness of the reaction to each demonstrated that the earlier causes were done for. Less than three weeks later Earth Day was celebrated, semiofficially crowning the crusade to protect us from our industrial society as the penultimate most urgent cause. Politicians and pundits informed us that we were not, after all, to be destroyed in racist warfare fought with hideous napalm bombs and fiendish nuclear weapons, as false prophets had previously taught; rather,

we would choke to death on polluted air and drown in a sea of polluted water, if poisoned food did not get us first.

Most of what government has subsequently passed off as consumerism and enviromentalism, of course, are merely old remedies in new bottles. The Interior Department, for example, still acts in accordance with its traditional pattern: when Democrats are in charge, it converts millions of acres of worthless privately owned land into national parks at great profit to Democratic land jobbers and great expense to the public, and when Republicans are in charge it practically gives away valuable publicly owned mineral lands to rapacious Republican exploiters. So, anyway, does the out-party always charge. The in-party, having always justified its conduct as conservation or resource management, still does; but now it describes its doings with such chic terms as environmental protection and ecological balance.

Similarly, the various federal guardians of our public health have modernized their language and tactics but are still, one suspects, peddling the same old panaceas. The Food and Drug Administration randomly and ruthlessly drives small-business men out of business at the first rumor of botulism in a batch of pizzas or chocolate bars, but nostrums are as plentiful and ineffectual as ever, and far more expensive than in the heyday of quack patent medicines. Too, the doings of the FDA have not been entirely untainted by hanky-panky. One of its more spectacular actions, for example, was the banning of cyclamates as a sugar substitute after a study by scientists at the University of Wisconsin demonstrated that cyclamates can cause cancer in mice. Not until much later did it come to light

that the dosages fed the laboratory animals were enormous: to ingest its equivalent, humans would have to drink 1300 bottles of cyclamate-sweetened soda pop a day. It also turned out that the Wisconsin study was financed by a grant from the American Sugar Institute. Despite these revelations, however, the ban on cyclamates remained in force.

The FDA and its equivalents in the state governments have, to be sure, enabled the medical profession to earn a tidy sum by requiring written prescriptions for a wide assortment of pills. This is good for the golf industry (doctors being traditionally that sport's main source of support), for to obtain the prescription the doctor's customers must submit to, or at least pay for, a medical examination. This procedure rarely causes physical harm to the patient, now and again saves him from taking a drug that would be harmful, and—or so it is rumored—has been known actually to help a patient.

In sum, most of what the older agencies do is hokum, but it is essentially harmless hokum, and some of it may even be beneficial. Life expectancy after early childhood, for instance, has increased by four or five years in the last half century, though most of the increase resulted from the discovery of penicillin, which the federal government kept a secret for several years. And if the cost of government's benefactions is sometimes high, the expenditure has kept a lot of people employed and has thus contributed to keeping the economy warm.

THE GENUINE CONSUMER ADVOCATES and environmentalists were not entirely conned by the antics of politicians

and bureaucrats—not because they are especially perceptive but because, like their spiritual ancestors the Puritans
and prohibitionists, they are entirely unable to compromise.
For all their zeal, however, they are unlikely to return us
to a pristine era when things worked and manufacturers
and merchandisers sold us an honest product for an honest
dollar. For the consumerists act on the basis of two prem-
ises, both unsound. They quite properly assume that the
needs of big business, big labor, and big bureaucratized
government are served without much concern for the needs
or wants of the consumer; but they mistakenly assume as
well that the powerful can do as they like. That is their
first grievous error: they fail to understand that these
institutionalized power blocs are themselves locked into
positions in which there is only minimal room for maneu-
vering. The consumerists' second error is their assumption
that the great mass of consumers can be enlightened and
organized into a viable fourth force which can make its
needs felt against those of the other three.

Most of what they have been able to accomplish is
therefore irrelevant when it is not absurd. A case in point
is what happened in the Federal Trade Commission after
an attack by Nader and his Raiders discredited the administration of that agency by Paul Rand Dixon. President
Nixon was more or less forced by Naderites to replace
Dixon with Caspar Weinberger—a legitimate, activist consumer advocate. Under Weinberger's zealous direction the
FTC began a crackdown on fraudulent or false and misleading advertising; and his successor has intensified the
campaign. One result has been that prize contests and
green stamps have fallen upon evil times as sales gimmicks.

Another is that toymakers such as Mattel and Topper have been stopped from "using deceptive advertising which unfairly exploits children" (fair exploitation of children, presumably, is still acceptable). Toothpaste peddlers can no longer claim that their product makes girls more "kissing sweet" than the toothpastes of their rivals, unless they can prove it, and Bayer has come under pressure for asserting that its aspirins are better than most others, since its ground for the claim is merely that its standards of purity are far higher than those required by the FDA.

The nadir of Naderism in advertising came when the FTC set out to protect the unsuspecting consumer against the unsubstantiated claims made on behalf of Mazda automobiles. Mazda hucksters had adapted a country-western song and come up with a delightful jingle: "Piston engines go boing, boing, Mazda engines go hmmmmm." The FTC demonstrated that piston engines don't *really* go boing, boing, and that Mazda engines, under stethoscopic examination, make a sound that is clearly distinguishable from hmmmmm. The advertisement was banned.

Another favorite goal of zealous consumerists is truth in packaging. Thanks to their efforts, we can now discern from a glance at the containers of most cereals and instant foods just how many gms and mgs of most known nutrients each package contains. (Honestly, now, even if you can guess that mgs means milligrams, do you have any idea how much that is?) We are also informed—here I quote from a box of Carnation Instant Breakfast, Chocolate Flavor—that a particular package contains "nonfat dry milk, sucrose, cocoa, corn syrup solids, lactose, isolated soy protein, sodium caseinate, magnesium hydroxide, lecithin, sodium ascorbate, ammonium carrageenan, sodium silico aluminate, artificial flavors (including vanillin and ethyl vanillin), ferric orthophosphate, vitamin A, vitamin E acetate, niacinamide, calcium pantothenate, manganese sulfate, basic copper carbonate, pyridoxine hydrochloride, thiamine mononitrate, riboflavin, folic acid, and potassium iodide." (It is the ammonium carrageenan, of course, that tips off the alert consumer.)

Packaging need not, of course, be so technical; if anyone actually knew what we can ingest safely and consistently with our health, the information could readily be imparted in the mother tongue. But there is the rub: the state of scientific knowledge regarding nutrition and the effects of drugs on the human body is primitive, confused, and contradictory. This does not particularly upset the Naderites, for they are as impatient with undesired reality as are Jesus freaks and John Birchers, and get around it the same way, namely by refusing to believe it. Accordingly, they demand that the doctor, advertiser, grocer, and druggist do likewise, and get on with the business of telling us what is and is not good for us.

The fact of the matter is that we have a plethora of guardians of our weal, including the FDA, various divisions of the Department of Agriculture, a host of new consumer-protection commissions, two dozen other agencies of the federal government, the innumerable committees of the American Medical Association and the American Dental Association, and state boards that regulate the licensing and activities of doctors and pharmacists. We are polluted with health information even as we are polluted by noise and noxious fumes, and the consumerists cry for more.

One common reaction to this information overkill is faddism, for published medical opinion can be used to justify almost any regimen imaginable. Another is to ignore all medical advice. We have been warned for years that cigarette smoking is detrimental to our health, and we smoke more and more; we have been warned for an even longer time that being overweight is deadly, and we go right on gorging ourselves.

Underlying consumer resistance to doing what is best for one's self is a deep-rooted trait that neither Nader and all his Raiders nor Madison Avenue and all its minions can change. Long before either of these groups of persuaders came upon the scene, it was firmly embedded in our national character that it is unmanly to show concern over one's health and un-American to haggle over prices. For four decades there has been available to all Americans a shrewd and—as far as I am aware—incorruptible organization known as the Consumers Union, publishers of an excellent journal called *Consumer Reports*. Subscribing to the magazine and following its advice, however, has usually been practiced in private, like a hidden vice: nobody wants his friends to think he is a hypochondriac or a cheapskate.

LIKE ALL CRUSADERS, of course, the consumer advocates have a solution for the problem of resistance to salvation, namely the sword. The wildest-eyed of them—such people as Richard O. Simpson, chairman of the new Federal Consumer Product Safety Commission—propose to deal directly with the consumer by banning all products and putting smokers and other sociopaths in jail. The more sober, including Nader himself, look to where the leverage is, or rather seems to be, and therefore direct their attacks upon big corporate business. Nader's Center for the Study of Responsive Law has produced some eighteen books, representing its findings on a wide range of subjects, and (in addition to never getting their facts quite straight) they all share two things in common: hostility toward business and abysmal ignorance of it. In one of the Center's reports, *The Consumer and Corporate Accountability*, Nader himself has provided us with a handy "Citizen's Guide to the Economy," which might alternately be styled the Lewis Carroll school of economics.

For openers, Nader and his co-consumerists fail to understand that money costs money. At one point in his denunciation of the "controlled market," for example, Nader recites a list of technological wonders that might be ours ("can openers that prevent tiny metal fragments from falling into the can's contents, safer power lawn mowers . . .") but for the barrier imposed by "existing capital commitments or ways of doing business." Citing a specific example, he chastises the steel industry for not adopting the basic oxygen furnace until 1963, when it had been invented in 1950. But United States Steel alone had nearly $3 billion invested in existing open-hearth technology, on which the annual cost of interest and depreciation was $790 million. Had it scrapped its old equipment and replaced it with the new, it would still have been required to bear the cost of servicing and amortizing the original investment. Given everything, the basic oxygen furnace was therefore economically less efficient than the open-hearth. Only gradually, as old equipment wore out or as demand increased—and in the fifties steel companies were producing at little over 50 percent of capacity—was it feasible to make the change.

Secondly, the consumer advocates fail to realize that American business, far from having a free hand to do as it pleases, is almost suffocated by an excess of regulation. No less than seventy-four different federal agencies regulate the energy supply; more than twenty regulate water power; whole legions have a hand in regulating transportation. The way the regulatory snarl hampers legitimate efforts of business can be illustrated with the saga of Peoples Gas Company of Chicago, which unfolded over the course of two decades and came to a climax in the 1960s. Peoples Gas has a history of good management, it was combating air pollution before Ralph Nader was born, and it has striven mightily (and usually successfully) to bring its customers the highest quality of service consistent with the lowest possible costs. Toward the end of World War II its properties were rather diverse, and it was being leaned on by the Securities and Exchange Commission to reduce itself to a "single integrated utility property" in compliance with the Wheeler-Rayburn Act. To oversee the integration it brought in as chairman James F. Oates, a brilliant lawyer and seasoned veteran of dealing with regulatory agencies. The effort took many years and countless separate transactions and operations—every one of them approved in advance, after lengthy hearings, by the SEC, the Federal Power Commission, the Illinois public utility commission, the federal and state courts, and sundry other guardians of the public. At last the integration was completed, and Oates retired, satisfied that his life's work had been a success. Within a year the Justice Department brought suit against the company on the ground that the integration violated federal antitrust laws.

A third weakness in the consumerists' economics is a pathetic faith in the efficacy of decentralization and competition in industry. Nader quotes with approval an ingenuous estimate by the FTC, that if the antitrust laws were so enforced that the four largest firms in any industry controlled no more than 40 percent of the industry's sales, prices would automatically fall by 25 percent or more, and quality would be increased into the bargain. I do not know where the FTC got its figures; I suspect that, like Lucy in the comic strip *Peanuts*, it just made them up. In any event, the proposition is palpably nonsensical for such capital-intensive industries as electric and gas utilities and mass transportation, and in many others (the metals industries, for instance) capital costs in relation to total market are so high that there is simply no room for more than a handful of major companies. As for those industries which are in fact within the range of the FTC's 40 percent formula, most rank high among the environmentalists' and consumerists' lists of polluters and profiteers—coal, petroleum, drugs, food, trucking, and so on.

Any blanket indictment of business on the basis of size alone is absurd. Big grocery chains supply food better and cheaper than do corner stores; that is why they are big. Big packers can produce safer meat than the country butcher, for they can afford the necessary investment in sanitation equipment. Gigantic lumber companies like

Weyerhaeuser and Georgia-Pacific can and do follow conservation practices that the little lumberman cannot and does not, for they can afford it and it is in their interest to do so. In sum, those who like Ned Ludd would break up the machine, physical or institutional, are woefully ignorant of what the world was like before the machine came along.

And there is one more thing. Nader, along with most environmentalists and many politicians, believes that corporate profits are both wicked and unlimited, and proposes to make corporations pay for every manner of social benefaction by dipping into them. Senator William Proxmire wants the steel industry to curb inflation by cutting prices rather than raising them, and absorb the loss out of profits; Nader wants the industry to rectify an unfavorable balance of trade by selling steel below cost in foreign markets, also absorbing the loss out of profits. The fact is that profits are too small to absorb much of anything. In the bonanza year 1972, U. S. Steel earned $200 million on gross sales of $5.4 billion, meaning that its pretax profits were 3.7 percent of sales; its profits after taxes were 2.8 percent of sales.

Big Steel's profit rate happens to coincide almost exactly with that of American industry as a whole, and like that of industry as a whole it is steadily declining. In 1965 U. S. Steel netted $519 million on sales of $4.4 billion, or 11.7 percent. General Motors netted $2.1 billion on sales of $20 billion that year, or 10.5 percent, and in 1972 netted the same $2.1 billion on sales of $30 billion, or 7 percent. To put it differently, Steel had to gross an extra billion in 1972 to make less than half as much money as it had made seven years earlier, and General Motors had to gross an extra $10 billion to keep its earnings the same. To put it still another way, if these companies sold their products *at cost*, the price of hot rolled sheet steel could be cut from $171 to $166 a ton, and the price of a new Oldsmobile could be cut from $5496 f.o.b. Detroit to $5167.

To which an ardent consumerist would reply, "So what? They've made so much by gypping us so long, it's time they had a turn." That is the most naïve proposition of them all, for it betrays a total lack of comprehension of what profit is. Profit, like money, is a sociocultural invention whereby we measure something, though like money it is a yardstick that has a life of its own. No matter how it is reckoned, however, it is a reliable gauge for calculating what we get from what we do. If a particular company continues to produce goods and services worth less than those it consumes, its books show losses instead of profit, and it perishes—or rather it did before we invented the no-fail economy. If a whole society continues to produce goods and services worth less than those it consumes, it too perishes—and from this reality there is no escape.

FINALLY, the consumerists and the environmentalists are doomed to fail because, like most Americans, they do not understand the principle of diminishing returns. The principle can be illustrated by reference to the problem of reducing poisonous emissions from automobile exhausts. The first 60 percent of the emissions can readily be eliminated with minor tinkering and equipment costing less than $100 per car. The next $100 will eliminate another 20 percent, to a total of 80. The next $100 will take care of an additional 7 percent, and the next 3 percent more. At that point the curve goes almost straight up: each additional $100 in costs improves emission controls less than the last. The same principle applies to fuel economy: beyond a certain point, the addition of emission controls (and of safety devices) reduces engine efficiency at a rapidly increasing rate.

The American social and economic system has a built-in check against exceeding the point of diminishing returns. The check is implicit in the slogan "the greatest possible good for the greatest possible number," and the business enterprises that have been most successful are those that approximated that goal. Notice that it entails a sacrifice of quality for the sake of quantity and vice versa, and the sacrifice is greater as one moves toward one extreme or the other. We could insist that all automobiles be emission-free and of Rolls-Royce quality, but only the very rich could afford them. We could insist that medical care be free to all, but its quality would be unspeakably low. American business, for the most part, is designed to steer the middle course—to provide as much quality as is consistent with the tastes and pocketbooks of, say, the 70 percent in the middle ranges of the population.

The consumerists and environmentalists want it both ways, and that is simply not possible. Nader, for instance, wants us to enjoy all the benefits of a complex industrial society, but he also wants to abolish all forms of "structured power." Once, on a speaking tour, he had occasion to taste for the first time freshly squeezed juice from tree-ripened oranges. He waxed ecstatic over it, and vowed to begin a campaign to make it available to all Americans in place of the frozen pap that we buy in the grocery stores. Now, frozen juice is not as tasty or as wholesome as the fresh stuff, nor is any fruit or vegetable as good or healthful when it is frozen or picked green and shipped thousands of miles to ripen on the shelves. But most Americans can afford this admittedly inferior produce all year round, which was impossible before the advent of mass-produced fruits and vegetables and the development of the frozen foods industry. No doubt Mr. Nelson Rockefeller can afford to have fresh oranges flown in from Florida every morning if he likes, but what the rest of us have is about the best we are going to get—and is a great deal better than anybody else in the world ever had.

Here the real menace of consumerism and environmentalism begins to emerge. As a society we have a powerful urge for self-destruction, and the most common form that urge takes is to spread our bountifulness beyond its limits. In many areas of life—education and medical care, for example—we have already undermined all but the pretense to quality through "democratization" beyond the point of diminishing returns. The consumerists and the environmentalists cater to this weakness in our national character. If we follow their lead, we will only hasten the loss of what is left.

Chapter X

Not with a Bang,
but with a Whimper

NATIONS, LIKE INDIVIDUALS, sometimes equip themselves so heavily to prevent the recurrence of past unpleasantness that they become unable to deal with anything new. The French, for example, were magnificently prepared in 1940 to fight World War I, with the result that the Nazis were able to overrun them in less than six weeks; the United States, in the 1960s, was admirably prepared for World War II, and the disaster in Vietnam followed. So it is with the economy: the economy is running berserk and our institutional machinery, designed to prevent a recurrence of the Great Depression of the 1930s, is irrelevant when it is not positively detrimental.

Government, the most important single element in the economy, is helpless to do anything except possibly make things worse. Because manipulation of interest and tax rates is no longer effective in bringing about predictable ends, and because bureaucratic proliferation annuls efforts to police business and organized labor intelligently and in the public interest, government has lost most of its ability to regulate the economy. It remains vital as a consumer and redistributor of income, but in both capacities it is locked into policies it cannot undo. The principal components of federal government expenditures are defense, welfare, bureaucracy, subsidies, and interest; the principal components of state and local government expenditures are education and construction. In each of these areas except construction, the pressures for expansion, and therefore for inflation, are irresistible. Fat can be trimmed from the budget here and there, but in most instances waste is not only large but necessarily growing, and any attempt to cut it would be even more wasteful. Much of the defense budget is used to support soldiers who are not trained to fight, and most of the remainder goes for procurement of new guns, missiles, airplanes, ships, and tanks which are often no better and sometimes not as good as existing weaponry. Yet it is institutionally almost impossible to reduce the defense establishment—partly because of the lobbying power of both the armed forces and the defense producers, but also because of the need to keep the defense industries alive for future exigencies and the equally important need to maintain employment for the 350,000 engineers and other technical personnel, the 3.3 million other workers for whom the defense industries provide jobs, and the 2.5 million military and 1.2 million civilian personnel attached to the Defense Department. Phasing out these workers would entail social costs which, within the framework of our value system,

225

we simply cannot afford. Similarly, the interest bill could be cut but only by feeding the fires of inflation, and the bureaucracy could be cut but only by adding to the welfare rolls. Welfare and subsidies could be cut only at the price of social and political suicide. The education bill cannot be cut because of teachers' unions. Public construction could be cut, theoretically, but doing so would be to overcome the most powerful lobby apart from defense contractors and the agencies of government themselves. It would also involve doing away with a $20 billion annual business in building and maintaining highways, and throw another 2.5 million people out of work; and it is therefore entirely unlikely. In sum, government expenditures can go no way but up, and taxes obviously must go up with them.

In the nongovernment portion of the economy, the most important segment is devoted to the production and distribution of consumer durables—automobiles, furnishings, clothing, and appliances. In such industries the cost of compensating the technostructure is high, more or less fixed, and steadily expanding; the cost of labor is high, more or less fixed, and steadily expanding; and the cost of taxes, by contrast, is high, more or less fixed, and usually expanding. Only raw materials, among the significant parts of the total cost structure, vary directly with the volume of production. Accordingly, most producers of consumer durables set their prices on the basis of a "get-out point"; every dollar that sales fall short of that point is a dollar of net loss, and of every dollar they exceed that point roughly 75 cents is net profit. Both prices and the volume of production in such industries must therefore rise or else the companies involved must face shrinkage and (soon afterward) collapse. Moreover, to most of them expansion necessitates waste—in the form of built-in obsolescence, useless products, changes in fashions or styles, and the like.

In the area of consumer perishable goods, the main components of which are fuel and food, the steadily increasing level of wages and salaries both pulls and pushes up prices; and the nearly irreversible policies of the automobile industry in regard to the first and of the federal government in regard to both encourage waste as well as higher prices.

Service industries, including utilities and (what are virtually service industries) the petroleum companies and manufacturers of producer durables, are subject to most of the pressures that affect government and the consumer durable industries, and some others as well. In large measure their fortunes are dependent upon government and the consumer durable industries: aluminum and steel makers, for example, sell mainly to businesses which in turn supply something to government or the public. To be sure, the cost structures of the gasoline and metals industries, utilities, and other such businesses have long been relatively stable, mainly because they have sizable fixed costs in the form of interest and depreciation on large capital investments. But these businesses tend to compensate in wastefulness for the element of price stability they provide: the cost of replacing an obsolete steel furnace, refinery, or power plant is enormous, and so it is usually cheaper to stick with inefficient, fuel-devouring old equipment than to modernize.

227

What this comes down to is that prices are going to increase, taxes are going to increase, waste is going to increase, and unemployment is going to increase. Any effort to prevent the increase in any one of these four areas will, to the extent that it is effective, produce a corresponding acceleration of the increase in one or more of the others. Sporadically, dislocations will produce spectacular increases in one area or another, and these increases will be more or less permanent.

AND THERE WILL BE SHORTAGES—moderate and severe, short-lived and enduring, erratic and predictable. In 1973 the United States faced serious shortages of meat, grains, raisins, copper, cocoa, toilets, gasoline, fish, popcorn, paper, heating oil, natural gas, cabbage, cotton, electric power, silver, diapers, steel, chlorine, honey, and caskets.

Shortages are and will be of two kinds, physical and institutional. Some of the physical shortages are temporary and derived from natural causes; the shortages of raisins and popcorn, for instance, were directly due to weather conditions and were relieved with the harvesting of the next crop. Other items, especially agricultural products, were temporarily in short supply because of an interplay between unfavorable weather, government-imposed price ceilings and production limitations, and a sudden and large increase in worldwide demand. Still others, notably minerals and natural gas, were short because the world supply is limited and running out. Indeed, in the broadest terms, the world is short of most of the materials necessary for the functioning of modern industrial society.

That is something we are going to have to get used to. For a whole generation, Americans have been teaching the nonindustrialized peoples to aspire to our style and level of consumption, and in this madness we have been exceeded only by the Russians. The result has been a worldwide revolution in material expectations. Now the time has come when the United States, or somebody, is going to have to notify the Third World that we were mistaken, that there is not and can never be enough to go around. Most of us are not prepared to recognize this, and Americans from Richard Nixon to Ralph Nader blithely assume that technology will find an answer—without noticing that modern industrial technology's greatest feat is the destruction of natural resources on an unprecedented scale. But we will soon have to notice.

Which leads us to the other kind of shortages, the institutional. As technology defines what resources are, so also is technology in turn defined by the sociocultural and institutional framework in which it operates; an invention is worthless if nobody wants it, or it runs afoul of cultural prejudice, or it is incompatible with the existing institutional apparatus, or it is what engineers call "not economically feasible." There is enough silver in ocean water, for instance, to supply our industrial needs for centuries, but the cost of extracting it is prohibitive. Accordingly, for practical purposes that silver does not exist, and the shortage continues.

The way institutional forces interact to produce shortages is illustrated by the case of the paper industry. There is no shortage—just now—of timber, the main raw material used in making most paper, and the technology of the industry is efficient and advanced. But practically all paper mills in the United States and Canada are operating at full capacity, and yet paper of all sorts is in extremely short supply—hampering operations of packagers, publishers, grocery stores, and offices. If the increase in demand for paper could be stopped immediately, and if manufacturers should forthwith begin the construction of greatly expanded mill capacity, it would take two to four years to alleviate the shortage, for it takes that long to build new plants. But demand is not going to decline and the expansion of capacity is going to be slow if it comes at all.

The reasons are to be found in the recent history of the industry. Until 1970 papermakers had an excess of mill capacity, prices were low, and the profit rate in the industry was less than 3 percent of sales; and so there was no incentive for expansion. Then the industry began to be hit by antipollution laws and regulations, with the result that it was forced to spend more than a billion dollars on pollution control, which severely depleted its capital reserves and made it impossible to finance expansion out of accrued earnings. Then came the boom that began in 1971, pushing demand up toward full capacity— but profits, squeezed by rising costs, did not go up with sales. Simultaneously, the cost of money began to be forced upward. No manufacturer wants to borrow money at 10 percent and invest it in plants that will yield him 2.7 percent, and so the plants are not being built. Unless prices are allowed to rise astronomically, the shortage will continue and grow worse.

THE MOST CRUCIAL SHORTAGE of them all is that of fossil fuels, particularly petroleum. Like most other resources necessary to industrial civilization, fossil fuel is in short supply both in the physical and in the institutional sense. As to the physical, there is no shortage of self-styled experts talking glibly about hundreds of billions or even trillions of barrels of crude oil that probably lie deep in the bowels of the earth in such exotic places as the Amazon jungles, the Arctic and Antarctic regions, and the ocean floor. Until proved otherwise, however, such resources are like the silver in the sea—institutionally, economically, politically, or otherwise nonexistent.

In less fanciful terms, at the beginning of 1972 the United States had *proved* reserves of 38 billion barrels of recoverable oil in the ground; its proved resources of recoverable natural gas (1971) were 290 trillion cubic feet. Since American consumption of crude petroleum in 1970 was 3.5 billion barrels and consumption of natural gas was 22 trillion cubic feet, it appeared in the early seventies that domestic reserves amounted to nearly an eleven-year supply of crude oil and more than a thirteen-year supply of natural gas. That seemed quite adequate, in view of the rate explorers had been discovering new reserves: for several decades, despite an enormous increase in consumption, discovery of new reserves had kept pace with and actually even gained a little on consumption.

Even at that time, the figures were a bit misleading—to government officials, most businessmen, and ordinary citizens alike. For one thing, it was an open secret in the industry that gas producers, in order to obtain long-term financing, notoriously and unconscionably exaggerated their statements of reserves. For another, the figure for domestic reserves of crude oil included more than 10 bil-

lion barrels in Alaska (more than a fourth of the total)
and until the end of 1973 the Alaskan oil was unobtain-
able because environmentalist groups were able to block
construction of the pipelines necessary to make that oil
available. Nonetheless, there seemed to be no cause for
alarm as far as the actual physical resources were concerned.

Institutionally, however, problems were evident as early
as 1970. Traditionally, prices of gasoline and other petroleum products had been low and stable. Despite general
worldwide inflation, for instance, "regular" gasoline in
the United States had sold at an average retail price
around 31 cents a gallon for two decades and more. Fearing consumer resistance and (what was more frightening
to them) political action that would destroy their special
tax status, the major oil companies strove mightily to
keep the price at that level and still retain their profits.
Of the 31 cents retail price, about 17 cents was beyond
their control, since that much was eaten up in taxes and
fixed costs on investment, the remainder being costs of
crude oil (about 5 cents) and transportation, distribution,
and necessary dealer profits. For some time the major oil
companies were able to hold the line by making innovations in refining, transportation, and distribution techniques, but by the late 1960s the area of possible innovations had reached a point of diminishing returns, the
general rise in costs was beginning to take its toll, and the
profit margin was steadily disappearing. The only remaining area of flexibility was in the price of crude oil. To
capitalize on that flexibility, the majors turned increas-

ingly toward cheap and easily exploited foreign sources, especially those in Venezuela and the Arabic countries.

At that point, a variety of external pressures began to impinge upon the oil-refining industry. For one thing, independent producers and royalty owners' associations, greedy and possessed of immense political clout, deceived Presidents Johnson and Nixon by grossly overstating domestic oil reserves as a means of keeping import quotas low and thus keeping the price of domestic crude oil high. For another, after the catastrophic (and well-publicized) Santa Barbara oil spill in 1969, environmentalists were able to obtain legal curtailment of domestic exploration and development. For still another, in the wake of the Santa Barbara incident environmentalists were able to block the building of refineries in those eastern seaboard ports where the processing of imported crude oil would be most economical.

As a result of these and related forces, two quiet but profound changes occurred in the American oil industry in 1970 and 1971. One was that, for the first time in half a century, the discovery of new sources of domestic petroleum seriously lagged behind consumption. The other was a dramatic shift in the construction of refineries: the major oil companies rapidly expanded the building of refineries overseas and virtually stopped building them at home. Thus refining capacity inside the United States remained around 4.7 billion barrels a year from 1970 through 1973.

Given all that, the petroleum situation early in 1973 appeared to be as follows. The world total of proved reserves was 672 billion barrels, of which 335 billion (about 62 percent) were in the Mideast, nearly 100 billion bar-

233

rels (about 15 percent) were in the Soviet Union, and most of the rest were in the Americas. More important and more reliable for immediate purposes—or so it then seemed—were statistics on world production. The United States was producing about a fifth of the world's oil, the Soviet Union about 15 percent, Iran and Venezuela about 8 percent each, and Saudi Arabia, Libya, Trucial Oman, and Kuwait between 6 and 7 percent apiece; all told, these (the Big Eight) were producing about 80 percent of the world total.

From those figures, it seemed possible to obtain some notion of what the United States would soon be requiring from abroad. Left to its own resources, the United States might last four or five years, provided that its rate of increase of consumption could be held steady, and provided also that its overseas refining capacity was not subjected to foreign political interference. If American explorers were able to find new domestic reserves at a rate equal to existing consumption, and if consumption continued to accelerate no faster than it had through 1971, the United States would need to be importing the equivalent of all of Kuwait's production within eighteen months, all of Libya's five years later, and all of Saudi Arabia's four years after that.

That was the way things appeared early in 1973—before the crunch of cultural, political, ideological, and institutional reality demonstrated that the situation was even worse than it had seemed.

SORELY BESET as it is, the United States still has the strongest, most stable, and most nearly self-sufficient economy in the world. Moreover, solutions are available, not only to the energy crunch but also to the larger set of interlocked institutional problems of which the energy problem is only a symptom and a part. They are far from total solutions, and cannot prevent life in the United States from growing gradually, steadily, almost imperceptibly less tolerable, much as life in our great cities has grown. But the United States need not perish, as other great civilizations have perished before us.

Waste cannot be stopped, for example, but the problems arising from it and from the finiteness of the planet's resources could be staved off for a long, long time. One course that would help immensely would be simply to encourage the nonindustrialized portions of the world to remain nonindustrialized. They are not salvageable, anyway—or more properly, neither they nor we can hope to survive if we continue to insist that they follow the route traveled by the West. No small number of people believe that the Third World has a chance at survival only if its peoples are encouraged and abetted in following one variation or another of the path that Maoist China has taken. By that means they might be able to avoid starvation, and the long-range pressure on the resources necessary in industrial societies would be greatly relieved. Meanwhile, the United States might best serve itself and humanity by reserving its greatest asset—its capacity to produce food —for the exclusive use of the industrialized nations, or for the purpose of acquiring needed materials from the Third World.

Similarly, though inflation cannot be stopped, its most devastating effects could be minimized. The excess of

American dollars abroad and the related problem of the decline in the dollar's value are, in fact, in process of solving themselves, and will continue to do so if the federal government can repress its manic compulsion to interfere in every market process. The inflation rate in other industrial countries is higher than that in the United States, and trade imbalances are being rectified by a flow of foreign investment toward the United States as a result of the cheapness of the dollar. Sooner or later, if suitable international monetary and commercial agreements can be reached, the inflationary pressures in the industrial countries will reach a state of equilibrium. The day could be hastened—and immediate pressures on the United States could be appreciably reduced—if we were to cut by half, and perhaps more, the billions we are spending for military purposes in Europe every year.

In the matter of energy, it is imperative that we return to coal, mainly through steam-generated electricity, as our primary source of power. This would entail a wholesale shift toward electric-powered mass transportation, a phasing-out of trucking except on short hauls, and an abandonment of the automobile as it has so far been known. On the other hand, electric automobiles, powered by batteries for local driving and driven (and recharged) by central-station electric lines along existing superhighways—much in the way of the old-fashioned streetcars—are entirely feasible. Such a shift would take ten to twenty years, but it could still be accomplished if a start were made soon.

But neither these nor any other sweeping, fundamental solutions to our dilemma are likely to be implemented unless Americans undergo a drastic change in attitudes. Obviously we would have to abandon our traditional postures toward other nations. Part of this might be easy, for in the matter of whom to fear and hate we have always been quite flexible; but it will be less easy to abandon our self-image as savior of the have-nots of the world. The other requisite changes of attitudes would have to overcome three powerful and deeply rooted elements in the American psyche, each of which has been thoroughly institutionalized and thus made extremely resistant to change.

One of these is inherent in the scientific and technological mentality that made all our economic achievements possible in the first place, namely the problem-solving approach to things. The scientific method isolates problems and solves them: it cannot take the broader view, for anything beyond the immediately demonstrable, testable, measurable, and provable is by definition unscientific. Americans are parodies of the scientific mentality: when anything goes wrong, we fix it, and do not take into account the possibility that our principles may be unsound. If a tire with adequate treads goes flat, we look for a hole and plug it up; we rarely think of replacing the tire, even less commonly consider the possibility that inflated rubber might not be the best cover for wheels, and almost never think about substitutes for wheels. This psychic quirk enabled the United States to become the most proficient exploiter of technology the world has ever known; but the same mentality is a barrier to perceiving or dealing with fundamentals.

The second cardinal element in the American psyche is hostility toward business enterprise. Even as we applaud and encourage and boast about our material progress, we castigate the agents of that progress, the businessmen who have been its prime movers. Any list of the great creative Americans, in the economic sense, would have to include Alexander Hamilton, Nicholas Biddle, Jay Cooke, and Samuel Insull; and yet the heroes of American history and folklore are not these men, but the politicians who destroyed them. This should not, of course, be surprising, for Hamilton, Biddle, Cooke, and Insull were men outside the American mainstream: each succeeded by getting down to fundamentals, and each had therefore to be destroyed.

The third paralyzing element in the American makeup is related to the first two and in some respects is the most dangerous of all: it is our inability to believe that our wealth and particularly our natural resources are finite. That incapacity leads us, when we are confronted with devastating shortages of the natural resources which are indispensable to our way of life, to refuse to believe what we are seeing, and, instead, to denounce the crooked businessmen who must have been responsible for artificially creating the shortage. It also prohibits us from understanding what should be obvious, that a no-fail economy is ultimately self-destructive—and that, spread over the rest of the world, it is as deadly as a metastasized cancer.

AND so the jaws of the trap close: gigantic, world-encompassing, irresistible, inevitable. The closing started in the early sixties, when we began our most recent orgy of breast-beating and world-saving; it gained tremendous momentum late in the decade, when we indicted our society for poisoning the environment. The problem of pollution is real, posing a serious menace to the continuation of civilized human life; but our response to sudden awareness of it was predictably absurd and made solution far more difficult. No one proposed to wait even until a crash-program study of the environment could be made, so that we might have some notion of how serious the problem was, what caused it, and what we might do about it. Nor did anyone think to blame himself. Apropos of the air scare, I polled an undergraduate class of mine, and learned that my forty students had driven thirty-five automobiles an average of ten miles to campus that day, and would of course drive ten miles home the same evening. Thus seven hundred automobile-miles were used in conveying forty students to and from class on a single average day; and yet none of the students thought himself in any way responsible for the foul air that enveloped the area. Instead of considering either course—study or self-blame—the Americans acted with all the paranoia and arrogant self-righteousness they inherited from their recent past, and demanded punishment and action, *at once.*

What followed was a nightmare, one which we are just beginning to feel the effects of, but one which portends a thousand more soon to come. First off, Congress considered the matter. In keeping with the rules of their game, which ordain that the successful politician is he who most effectively capitalizes on a popular fancy, congressmen scurried to introduce antipollution bills. Senator Edmund Muskie of Maine, then considered a front-runner for the presidential nomination in 1972, got the most mileage out of the scare by introducing and taking credit for the Environmental Protection Act of 1970, which was aimed primarily at drastically reducing, by 1975 and 1976, the supposed harmful emissions from automobile exhaust fumes. President Nixon, not to be outmaneuvered, forthwith gave the act life by appointing William Ruckelshaus to head the Environmental Protective Agency; and Mr. Ruckelshaus, not to be caught napping, rejected the request of the automotive industry to be allowed to explore alternative means of producing "cleaner" engines, opined that the industry was stalling, and insisted that "clean" engines, as defined by the act, be developed by adding gadgetry to the conventional internal-combustion engine. The automobile manufacturers, caught as flat-footed in the role of scapegoat for the nation's ills as the utilities had been a generation earlier—and as the railroads had been a generation before that—set out to comply with the law and with the EPA's orders.

Nobody noticed, or paid any attention to, the two most important facts that bore upon the matter. The first was that it was mightily presumptuous to suppose that man, having inadvertently upset the ecological balance, could restore it by an act of will or an act of Congress. (As it turns out, for example, after having studied the subject a bit ecologists now think that six to ten times as much emission of gases harmful to humans comes from a wide range of "natural" causes—from belching cows to rotting trees—as come from man-made causes, and over these we have no controlling power at all. It also turns out, according to studies conducted by West German scientists, that emissions from the combustion of leaded gasoline, considered a menace in 1970, have a positively favorable effect on plant life, and therefore on the purity of the air.)

The second was that ecology rules, even in efforts to tamper with the ecological balance, for man himself is part of the ecological system. Nature compensates for everything man does or tries to do—and one of nature's most subtle devices is to blind man to the consequences of his actions. Hence the automotive industry started developing the required antipollution devices, and considered it only an unpleasant side effect that fuel consumption went up as emissions got cleaner. Moreover, automotive engineers (responding to the market, to the law, and to the institutional requirements of the industry) continued to add safety devices and power brakes and transmissions and windows and other gadgetry designed to make cars safer and more comfortable, and to add many pounds per vehicle into the bargain. Horsepower requirements necessarily went further up, and mileage per gallon of gasoline necessarily went further down. Chevrolets and Plymouths and Fords, which once had delivered 18 or 20 miles per gallon, and had slipped by the late sixties to around 15 miles per gallon, delivered less than 10 miles per gallon on their 1974 models, two years before the antipollution standards of 1976 were to be met. Nobody seemed concerned that the decline in efficiency would double the consumption of gasoline, even assuming that the level of travel should stay the same.

Meanwhile, the utility companies had been enjoying a false and short-lived sense of security. Everybody who knew anything about electric power had long recognized that (except for heating) it was far more efficient and scores of times as clean as any alternate source of energy, and foresaw a golden age in which virtually all motive power in the United States, including personal transportation, would come from central-station electric companies. Economically, technologically, ecologically, and even politically that seemed the only way things could go. And so, even when the automotive industry came under attack, the utility industry believed itself immune and continued to promote ever expanding uses of electricity. One important consequence of this attitude was the completion of the air conditioning of the South and Southwest, with vast socioeconomic ramifications in those areas: people there began to work with far more rather than far less energy than their northern brethren, and the nation's manufacturing became more scattered geographically, which in turn necessitated additional trucking and a concomitant increase in the waste of fuel. A second important consequence was that operators of large office buildings and factory spaces in the North, concerned about the effects of unclean air on their workers, designed and built air-conditioned buildings which had no windows. Buildings of twenty-five, forty, a hundred stories were erected, none of them having a way to let in fresh air, all requiring enormous amounts of energy. It seemed only sensible, except in the unthinkable event that electricity should become in short supply.

But short was the supply soon to become. In part the brownouts and blackouts of the summers of 1972 and 1973 arose from a long history of inept management, especially in the area between Philadelphia and the state of Maine, where electrical technology is generally on a par with the

Model T Ford and local politics reflects no great improvement over the days of Boss Tweed. In far larger part, however, shortages and impending shortages and dislocations were the product of popular crusades to "save the ecology" —crusades as downright ignorant as their motto. Various people with far more money than intelligence noticed that strip mining made the verdant hills of central Appalachia ugly, and so strip mining was outlawed—and by 1973 the area was actually importing coal. Meanwhile, various other people noticed that the burning of most grades of bituminous coal, however mined, emitted a great deal of sulfur into the air, and so legal restrictions were enacted to prohibit or punish the burning of such coal. Still others threw up barriers to the exploitation of the immense fields of relatively clean-burning soft coal in Montana. Not content, environmentalist groups tied up the efforts of electric utility companies to develop thermonuclear power plants. As a result of all this, a six hundred years' supply of soft coal and a practically infinite supply of thermonuclear energy institutionally ceased to exist, at least for the time. Electric utility companies began to turn, about 1970, toward alternative sources of fuels, which meant mainly oil derivatives and natural gas.

At this point still another institutionalized element, and then Mother Nature herself, entered the equation. The Federal Power Commission had long kept the price of natural gas extremely low, on the characteristically American ground that businessmen should not be allowed to make excess profits by supplying something that was more or less a public necessity. Accordingly, when electric utilities shifted away from coal they took gas in preference to heating oil whenever gas was available, even though gas is only about a third as efficient as either oil or coal. That strained the gas supply, and droves of homeowners and factories converted from gas to oil for heating. Then came the extraordinarily cold winter of 1972–73 and an impending shortage of heating oil. The major oil refineries met the shortage by turning out extra heating oil; but doing so required cutting back on production of gasoline. In spring they reversed their positions and increased the output of gasoline, partly to adjust to seasonal demand and partly because, given the snarl of government controls, gasoline was for the moment more profitable than heating oil. Consequently, heating oil was short again for the winter of 1973–74. After all, capacity is capacity, in oil refineries or anything else.

And the capacity was simply not there. All this came about just as the automotive industry—pushed by Ralph Nader's crusade, Senator Muskie's ambitions, President Nixon's counterambitions, Administrator Ruckelshaus' determination, and the industry's own institutional dictates —was vastly increasing the demand for nonbituminous fossil fuels. Refining capacity remained at 13 million barrels a day, and demand soared to 18 million barrels. On top of that, the Arabic nations, with a wave of a blackmailing sheik's hand, cut off the flow of Mideast oil.

In sum, everybody needed more natural gas and gasoline than there was available, and everyone wanted it at once. What was far more scary, everyone wanted more than there was in existence.

The consequence of this bizarre chain of events was

the creation of a incredible inflationary bottleneck. Bottle-necks, once relatively uncommon, are now entirely char-acteristic of our times: they occur when flukish circum-stances combine to produce a temporary shortage of and/or excess demand for a commodity or service, bringing a large temporary increase or a moderate permanent increase in price. What occurred in 1973 was the same phenomenon on a scale so grand that the effect of the bottleneck was explosive. The total demand pressure was indescribably powerful: in a manner of speaking, all the money in the world became involved in urgent bidding for a quite limited supply of gas and gasoline. And because the entire world economy was involved, the entire world economy would soon have to adjust to the disruption of cost struc-tures that an astronomical increase in fuel prices necessar-ily entailed. Once that took place, it would be virtually im-possible for anything to return to a precrisis "normal" ever again. Cheap fuel lay at the very base of technological civilization, and the era of cheap fuel was over.

THE LIST OF SHORTAGES grows longer. Food. Jobs. Elec-tric power. Paper. Minerals. Fuel. And the boom roars on.

Epilogue

A Parable

A DECADE OR SO AGO, in that bygone era in which Detroit was allowed to produce automobiles that would run, I owned a magnificent powder-blue Buick convertible. Each of the several thousand parts of that superb vehicle—every cam, every piston, every valve lifter and bearing—was the product of careful machine tooling and represented the culmination of the ideas and labor of generations of inventors and engineers. It devoured gasoline voraciously, but when one commanded it to go, with a gentle press of the foot, it took off with the smooth graceful power of a Boeing 707; and at a hundred miles an hour it was pure silk.

From time to time little things went wrong, but they were easily managed. The speedometer went out, but who needed one? Someone slashed the top, the power mechanism that operated the right rear window failed, the zipper on the celluloid rear window broke; but tape, baling wire, and safety pins minimized the effects of those problems. The welding on the catch that secured the front seat came undone, but I learned to brace myself in just the right way while braking, so that was only a trivial inconvenience. When winter came the heater proved defective, emitting noxious fumes, but blankets provided adequate protection on all but the coldest days. And compared to the seductive thrill of racing that great machine at a hundred miles per hour, these nuisances were minor, indeed.

As the years and the miles sped by, more serious problems began to develop. At one point the rubber hoses of the power braking system sprang a leak, the brakes failed, and I crashed into a culvert, twisting the frame and smashing the right fender and headlight. The repair bill would have been more than the car was worth, so I had the brakes fixed and the headlight replaced, and I was back on the road, moving smoothly if somewhat sideways, like a crab. Not long afterward, someone sideswiped me on the left side; the beautiful blue body was becoming pretty homely now. Then the oil gaskets in the engine sprang a leak, and soon the wonderful machine was consuming nearly as much oil as gas; but it was cheaper to buy oil than have the engine overhauled, and I did so.

By this time various friends, no doubt ashamed when I parked this beast in front of their homes, began to hint that maybe it was time for me to get a new car. But I would take them for a ride and show them why I would not change: noisy, uncomfortable, dangerous, and ugly as the old thing was, she was still silky smooth at a hundred miles an hour, and nothing on the road could match her for performance.

Then one fine day, when I cranked up this technological marvel, an idiot light came on, indicating that my oil pressure was defective. I cut the engine and telephoned my garage man, who told me not to attempt to drive the car: he would send a wrecker to haul it to the garage. Thinking that a mere 4-mile trip could do no harm to this best of possible machines that had survived all else, and thinking also to save a $10 towing charge, I spurned the advice and started out. Each of the thousands of parts, save the oil pump alone, did just what it was designed to do, for each could do no other. I made 3 miles, and then the engine, heated beyond imagination by running without lubrication, ceased entirely to be an engine, and all those finely tooled parts ceased to be parts: under the hood there was nothing but a single, immovable mass of fused metal. The car stopped dead, never to go again.

Index

AAA (Agricultural Adjustment Administration), 106, 118, 122–23, 147
Abrams, Richard, 61
Adams, Henry, 15, 16, 60
Advertising: consumer movement and, 213–16; institutional, 92
Affluence (prosperity), 2–11, 12–37, 157 (*see also* Profits; Wealth); anticommercialism and, 38–58, 59–81, 82–101, 102–25, 126; no-fail economy and, 152–77; welfare capitalism and (*see* Welfare capitalism)
AFL (American Federation of Labor), 112, 113, 186
AFL-CIO, 186
Aggregate demand, 153–54; shortages and, 226–38
Agrarian republicanism (agrarian tradition), 44–47, 49, 56–58, 69, 77
Agriculture (farmers), 44–46; agrarian tradition and, 44–47, 49, 56–58, 69; crop restrictions and, 8–9; New Deal and, 106, 118, 119, 121, 122–23; subsidies, 122–23, 147–49
Air conditioning, 242
Aircraft industry, 175–77
Air pollution. *See* Antipollution
Alaska pipelines, 232
Aluminum Corporation of America (Alcoa), 140–44
Aluminum industry, 140–44
American Car and Foundry, 130
American Economic History, 55
Americanization, 86
American Telephone & Telegraph, 32, 91
Anticommercialism (antibusiness movement), 38–58, 59–81, 82–101, 102ff., 201, 237–38; consumer and environmental movements and, 204–23, 237–38; radicalism and, 56–58, 59–81, 82–101, 102–25, 126–51, 178–79, 189
Antipollution movement, 171–74, 202, 204–5, 211, 215–23, 230, 238–43
Antitrust laws and enforcement, 33, 65, 70–75, 116, 146, 219
A&P Company, 116, 127
Appalachian whites, organized labor and, 186–88
Armour and Company, 66, 72, 85

Arnold, Thurman, 116
Atomic Energy Commission, 146
Automobile use, 2, 5–6 (*ese also* Automotive industry); and fuel shortages, 2, 5–6, 7–8, 236, 244
Automotive industry, 1, 4, 18–19, 64, 139, 145, 196, 246–48 (*see also* Automobile use; specific companies); consumer and environmental movements and, 205–10, 214, 220–23, 239, 240–42, 244; costs and prices, 226, 227; emission standards, 171–74; and unions, 114, 115, 179–80, 181, 182–85

Baker, George F., 77
Bankruptcy Act (1934), 33
Banks (banking), 28–32, 65–66, 70, 77–79, 92–101 (*see also* Capital); and interest rates, 6–7; New Deal and, 103, 128–32
Bank of the United States, Second, 46, 47–48, 49
Barton, Bruce, 91
Baruch, Bernard M., 79–80
Belmont, August P., 29
Bessemer (Henry) and Bessemer process, 25
Biddle, Nicholas, 46, 238
Bigness (big business), 40–41; anticommercialism and (see Anticommercialism); consumerism and, 219–21; New Deal and, 102–25, 126ff.; reforms and, 59ff.; "wheeler-dealers" and, 126–51
Black Americans, 110, 119, 122; organized labor and, 186–88, 189
Blough, Roger, 147
Bolingbroke, Henry St. John, Viscount (and Bolingbrokism), 39–42, 43, 47, 48, 58, 103, 104, 111, 201
Bonds, corporate, 29–30, 31–32, 95–97; utility, 95–97
Bribes. *See* Corruption (bribery, graft)
Bryan, William Jennings, 57, 69, 104, 201
Bureau of Corporations, 71, 74
Bureaucracy (civil service), 138, 160–77, 225–26; organized labor and,

251

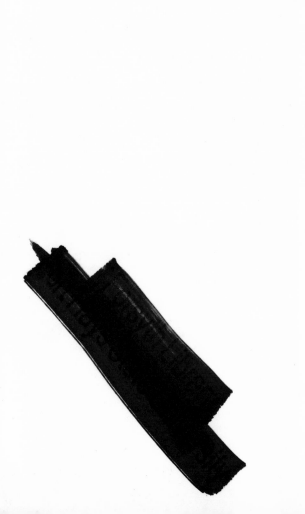